W9-APJ-932

DESERT HIKING

DESERT HIKING

DAVE GANCI

Wilderness Press
Berkeley

Copyright © 1979 by Trend Books; 1983, 1987 by Dave Ganci

SECOND EDITION March 1987
Second printing November 1988
Third revised printing January 1991

Cover design by Larry Van Dyke
Library of Congress Card Number 87-50103
International Standard Book Number 0-89997-086-9
Manufactured in the United States of America
Published by Wilderness Press
        2440 Bancroft Way
        Berkeley CA 94704
        (415) 843-8080
        Write for free catalog

Library of Congress Cataloging-in-Publication Data

Ganci, Dave.
   Desert hiking.

   Bibliography: p.
   Includes index.
   1. Desert survival. 2. Hiking. 3. Backpacking.
4. Hiking--Southwestern States. 5. Backpacking--
Southwestern States. I. Title.
GV200.5.G36 1987   796.5'1'0979   87-50103
ISBN 0-89997-086-9

To Kes, who left it up at the high camp.

With special thanks to Sara Baird, Peter Baird, Roger Kaufman, and Linda Taylor.

Contents

Foreword

"An earnest love of Nature, even in her grimmest and sullenest moods, made me look forward with delight to the deserts of the Southern route; and my anticipations were realized. Tramping month after month across the great empire of Texas; then wandering free and glad beneath the skies of Arizona and New Mexico; beholding now and then the flag of the Republic, flaunting in its wide authority over those lonesome and hungry wastes of the Middle Continent—this is a pleasure, to be fully enjoyed only by the pedestrian. These were the happiest days of my life, and there comes to me sometimes an insatiable longing to roam again, in the large liberty and lawlessness of the prairies, and to grapple once more with the savage deserts."

The above was taken from *Afoot and Alone,* a nineteenth-century account of a cross-country trek undertaken by Stephen Powers. He began his journey at Raleigh, North Carolina, on New Year's Day, 1868. After walking 3,556 miles, he arrived at San Francisco eleven months later.

Preface

Backpacking in the desert is a joy. Wildlife is everywhere, if
you take the time to look for it. Wildflowers and exotic plants
spread out in all directions and in all seasons. Sunrise pinks
and greens, noonday yellows, and sunset purple-browns provide a daily kaleidoscope of color. Desert storms are mind-
boggling blitzkriegs of cumulous clouds, rain, thunder, and
electricity dissipating into clear, constellation-counting nights.
The desert landscape guides the eye to forms of long, soft
shadows broken by sharp, dry, desert peaks. Archaeologists are
still discovering remnants of past societies that are hiding in
washes, cliff sides, and earth mounds. The desert is a museum
of contrast and variety offered to the foot traveler at a price:
thoughtful planning, respect for the land, and a sense of
responsibility toward future generations.

This book is a guide to get you started in your accumula-
tion of knowledge and experience. It should help equip you
for a safe and enjoyable sojourn into the lands of little water.
Whether you are a beginner contemplating your first day hike
or an old-timer with a fifty-pound load on your back, there is
no substitute for personal experience; therefore, I have in-

cluded some of the lessons that I and some other hikers have learned from experience. You will find out that there are few absolutes in desert backpacking save sun, sand, and solitude. I have mentioned some "shoulds" although ultimately you will have to make all the decisions yourself. After all, one of the ideas in getting out in the first place is to express your individuality, creativity, and self-sufficiency. To do that, you have to learn some things by trial and error.

During my thirty years of experience with backpacking, I have listened to the advice of self-styled "experts," backpacking "bibles," the National Safety Council, and *Consumer Reports*. They all have axes to grind—or sell. You can learn some principles from them and from books like this one. Then you must modify everything to suit your own goals and personality. Take the knowledge from this book and experiment. You may be able to improve on many of the techniques given here. I won't bog you down with a myriad of details to cover every conceivable situation. My goal is to provide you with enough information and inspiration to step away from the roadhead full of confidence and excitement (Watch out for that dead cholla cactus!) and drink in the clear air of the arid environment (after you've taken that long, last drink from the five-gallon water container you keep in the car).

Colin Fletcher, at one point along the river during his fantastic walk through the Grand Canyon, shed all his clothes but hat, boots, and pack, and continued walking merrily along, no doubt startling the desert wildlife with his audacity. Now that's confidence!

So let's get with it. Read this guide along with some books on desert natural history. Spend some time in a desert museum or botanical garden. Then truck on out. And remember, if there were only three things you could carry into the desert, they would be water, water, and more water.

1

What Is A Desert?

. . . How come everything out there either stinks, sticks, or stings?

Everything seems to be at war in the desert. The plants are continually defending themselves with spines, spikes, stabs, needles, claws, saw edges, hooks, and daggers. Insects stink, sting, bite, chew, pinch, or just hang on. We fight back with walking sticks, lug-soled boots, long sleeves, curse words, and Off.

That's one way that I sometimes describe the desert. Certainly you will come up with a few choice words of your own after you've stomped around out there once or twice. In the meantime, here are a few comments on the desert collected from various sources.

"A desert is an area in which bare earth is the most conspicuous feature of the landscape."

David E. Costello

"A God-forsaken wasteland, that's what it is."

> Tourist whose car broke down in
> Desert Center, California

"Ours has been the first and will doubtless be the last party of whites to visit this profitless locality. It seems intended by nature that the Colorado River, along the greater portion of its lonely and majestic way, shall be forever unvisited and undisturbed."

> Lieutenant Joseph Christmas Ives,
> who in 1857 led the first government
> exploration of the Grand Canyon
> Desert

"A desert is a region in which the evaporation during the year exceeds the precipitation during the year."

> Audubon Institute of Desert Ecology,
> 1973

"Although individual parts of these arid regions are quite different in physical appearance, they possess in common several characteristics, such as low rainfall, high average temperatures during the day, and almost constant winds, with consequent increased rate of evaporation."

> Edmund C. Jaeger

"What do we want from these vast worthless areas—this region of savages and wild beasts, of shifting sands and whirlwinds, of dust, cactus, and prairie dogs? To what use could we ever hope to put these great deserts and those endless mountain ranges?"

> Daniel Webster

"The desert is a fragile land. It needs to be respected for what it is, rich and varied and beautiful in its own way. It must no longer be regarded as land that God never quite got around to finishing."

Ruth Kirk

"It has so many physical forms that flora and fauna are more numerous and varied than in many of our luxuriant forests."

David E. Costello

"Once the desert environment is understood, it loses its mystery. The great open desert soon grows to be a friendly place with an ever-changing beauty of shifting color and shadow. It becomes a joy to view its vast distances to bordering mountains, painted in sunset and sunrise colors; its landmark of wells, trails, habitations, and salt lakes; its hills emerging from the desert plain as from a sea. The scurrying lizards and hardy plants belie the conception of the desert as a barren waste. And, once or twice a year for a few weeks after a rain, brilliant red, orange, and white flowers outdo the brown and yellow of rock and sand. Then the desert is a garden spot with hovering insects and the scent of blossoms. Especially at night is the desert serene and friendly; the stars stud the sky, or the landscape is flooded with moonlight."

The Rochester Desert Unit from "Physiology of Man on the Desert"

"There is something infectious about the magic of the Southwest. Some are immune to it, but there are others who have no resistance to the subtle lures and who must spend the rest of their lives dreaming of the incredible sweep of the desert, of great golden mesas with purple shadows, and tremendous stars appearing at dusk from a turquoise sky. Once infected, there is nothing one can do but strive to return again and again.

From *Prehistoric Indians of the Southwest,* by H. M. Wormington

"Of all the trouble I had on my 15-day, 83-mile survival walk across the Arizona desert in July—lack of water, living off the land, 120° heat, dry water holes, hepatitis, torn clothing, little shade—the thing that liked to drive me crazy were those damned 'fast ants' that squeezed through the mosquito netting of my tent to zoom across my naked dehydrated body, looking for God knows what."

Peter Busnack, carpenter and founder
of "Reevis Mountain School of
Self Sufficiency."

North American Deserts

The North American deserts cover approximately 500,000 square miles and are inhabited by fantastic adaptations of living forms that require little rainfall. From southern Washington state to the tip of Baja California, over to the middle of Mexico, this sometimes harsh, sometimes lush land supports varieties of plant and animal life that have evolved over millions of years. The vertical boundaries of the deserts range from 280 feet below sea level in Death Valley to 5,000 feet above sea level in the Great Basin. Rainfall is scant. There is a high evaporation and temperature rate, a high soil temperature, and a great amount of radiation. That's why you can cook an egg on your car hood in Gila Bend, Arizona, in July.

Scientific estimates are that our present deserts were formed anywhere from 5 to 60 million years ago when the Sierra Nevada and Cascade Mountain ranges were rising up. During the interim, four glacial ice ages came and melted away leaving great inland seas. The Great Salt Lake in Utah is one remaining example. Prehistoric animals like elephants, bison, great sloths, saber-toothed tigers, dire wolves, and other now-extinct beasts roamed these areas.

Among the many factors responsible for creating the deserts were circulation patterns of the atmosphere, rain shadow effects, the distance from ocean moisture, and cold ocean currents. The Sierra Nevada and Cascade Mountains create the

General desert flora, growing in the Lower Sonoran. Courtesy of the Desert Botanical Gardens, Phoenix, Arizona.

rain shadow effect for the Great Basin and some of the Mohave Desert by draining all the moisture from clouds moving easterly from the Pacific. As the moisture dissipates into the mountains, the hot dry air that characterizes the arid climate forms the desert lands on the leeward side of the ranges. The Sonoran Desert of southern Arizona and north-western Mexico is created by this rain shadow also.

Another cause for the dry land environments is the more or less permanent descending dry air characteristic of the desert locations in the "horse latitudes"—latitudes too far north of the equator to get any tropical rainfall and too far ·south to catch moisture from ascending cool air. That's why you can hike in the Arizona desert in shorts in December when you need a snowplow just to find your car in New York.

Some rainfall does reach all of the North America deserts. As a rule, winter rains fall in the northern and western portions of the desert while the southern areas receive both winter and summer storms. Summer storms blow up from the Gulf of Mexico and reach inland as far as central Arizona.

The following descriptions will acquaint you with the geography of the six major desert regions of North America. You'll find more information about specific parks, monuments, gardens, museums, wilderness areas, and other points of interest for each of these desert areas in Appendix 1. Appendix 2 lists several books that can tell you still more about your favorite landscape.

Great Basin

The Great Basin is the coldest, highest, largest, and northern-most of the North American deserts (see map, page 158). It covers most of Nevada and Utah and extends into southeastern Oregon, southwestern Idaho and Wyoming, the northwestern corner of Colorado, and a small portion of northern Arizona. Due to its more northern location, the Great Basin has lower temperatures and shorter summers. Most of it stands over 4,000 feet above sea level and periods of freezing are not uncommon in winter. Rainfall varies from 4 to 11 inches a year.

Because the Great Basin is so variable, you should find out as much as possible about the specific area you wish to explore, especially the high and low temperatures that can be expected. Then plan accordingly.

Great Basin vegetation is characterized by grey green sagebrush and shadscale, low-lying shrubs that cover hundreds of square miles in continuous sweeps. Cacti are small and sparse. Willows and cottonwoods occur along streambeds. Wild flowers and grasses show up whenever favorable moisture and temperature conditions coincide. Juniper and pinyon trees are found at the higher elevations.

Unobstructed views for hundreds of miles, clean and clear sky, rugged mountains, and untouched stretches of open country greet the hiker. There are few rivers in the Great Basin, but the area is enhanced by many lakes, including the Great Salt Lake, Pyramid Lake, and Honey Lake. Spectacular sand dunes are found north of Winnemucca, Nevada.

Pronghorn antelope, mule deer, jackrabbits, ground squirrels, badgers, skunks, mice, and other ground dwellers share this area with the resident sage grouse and the many migratory birds that frequent the inland lakes.

Mohave Desert

The Mohave Desert, situated primarily in southeastern California, is somewhat of a transition zone between the Great Basin to the north and the Sonoran Desert to the south. It contains the famous Death Valley, although most of its territory stands between 2,000 and 4,000 feet in elevation.

The Sierra Nevadas dominate the western skyline with parallel mountain ranges. Dry alkaline lakebeds form the eastern boundaries. The Colorado River runs through the southeast section and on into the Sonoran Desert.

Average rainfall varies from two inches on the eastern border to five inches in the west and falls during the winter

(Above) Palm trees of Mohave Desert Canyons. Courtesy of the Desert Botanical Gardens.

(Left) Joshua tree, Yucca brevifolia, *in the Mohave Desert. Courtesy of the Desert Botanical Gardens.*

and spring months. Mountains are snow-capped in winter.

Creosote bush with its beautiful resinous scent dominates the Mohave plains. But the distinctive profile of the Joshua tree is the Mohave trademark. This tree is the center of life for much of the desert's fauna including screech owls, wrens, flycatchers, wood rats, snakes, and the desert night lizards.

Sonoran Desert

The mental picture most people get when they think of an American desert is the Sonoran Desert. Its picture-postcard saguaro and barrel cactus cover southwestern Arizona, Baja California, and the northwestern coast of Mexico. It is an area subject to a variety of climatic conditions. The area around the head of the Gulf of California is very arid. The western part of the Sonoran receives rain only during winter and spring, while the eastern part receives summer monsoon rains

Lower Sonoran Desert flatland and low mountains. Photo by Aimee Madsen.

Jumping cactus, Opuntia fulgida. *Common in the Lower Sonoran Desert. Courtesy of the Desert Botanical Gardens.*

due to storms over the Gulf of Mexico. But the eastern section also receives about an equal amount of rain in the winter, bringing the annual total to an average of ten to twelve inches.

The lush deserts of the Santa Catalina and Rincon areas near Tucson are magnificent museums of desert wildlife and plant life.

The Saguaro National Monument of southeastern Arizona is high on my priority list of desert hiking areas. Divided into two sections, east and west of Tucson, it has trails that take the explorer from the desert scrub communities up through the grassland transition, oak woodland, ponderosa pine forest, and Douglas fir forest in one day. But the distinctive feature of Sonoran plant life is the variety of spiny things called cactus. More than sixty species have been listed for Arizona. The Desert Botanical Garden in Phoenix is world renowned for its displays of cacti. Trees of the Sonoran include ironwood, mesquite, palo verde, and the giant upside down carrot called the boojum tree that grows along the Pacific Coast of Baja California. Dr. Forrest Shreve, who for many years was on the

Prickly pear cactus, Opuntia phoeacantha, *in the Lower Sonoran Desert. Courtesy of the Desert Botanical Garden.*

Machaerocereus eruca, *found along the beaches of Baja California. Courtesy of the Desert Botanical Garden.*

Young saguaro amid creosote bush and bursage on Lower Sonoran Desert. Photo by Dave Ganci.

staff of the Carnegie Institute's Desert Laboratories at Tucson, divided this desert into seven subdivisions based solely on species of plant life.

The variety of fauna coincides with the plant life variety. A visit to the Arizona-Sonora Desert Museum near Tucson is a unique experience. It is a desert zoo with nearly all the animals exhibited in their natural habitats. It is one of the foremost living museums in the world.

In August of 1973 I spent ten days at a National Audubon

Society desert ecology seminar at the base of the Rincon Mountains near Tucson. Professors of geology, botany, ornithology, herpetology, and invertebrates taught us the interrelationships of their respective disciplines and how this applied to the special adaptations of desert-living creatures. I learned to really "see" the desert for the first time, by stopping and standing still and watching. We picked out a plot of ground and observed it from early morning until evening. An unbelievable variety of animal life passed through each plot, from velvet ants to coyotes. Birds were everywhere, flitting from bush to cactus to tree to ground. Lizards, rodents, and insects of all kinds were doing their early-morning shopping and hunting, only to disappear when the ground heated up—just as we did, back to our cabins. As shadows lengthened, activity picked up, and after sundown the night life started and the after-hour creatures made their appearances (see Chapter 10, "A Day on the Desert"). After the first few days, I began to look at myself as a member of the desert community rather than just an objective viewer. I began to *feel* friendly toward the desert and its fragility. This is what can happen to you if you spend a vacation in desert wilderness. You will be hooked.

Chihuahuan Desert

The Chihuahua Desert covers southwestern Texas, southern New Mexico, and north central Mexico.   Elevations range between 3,000 and 6,000 feet. Freezing temperatures are common in the winter. Most of the rain falls in the summer, ranging from 3 to 12 inches, depending on the section. The Chihuahuan is not as extreme in its dryness as the other four deserts.

Hiking through this desert you'll find creosote bush, mesquite, tarbush, yucca, agave, and sotol. Small species of cacti mingle with a few trees, mainly along water courses. Elevation differences mean animal life variety, and this holds true for

(Left) Hedgehog cactus, Coryphantha erecta, *of the Southern Chihuahuan Desert Region.*

(Below) Another Southern Chihuahuan Desert beauty, Lemaireocereus dumortori.

Yucca, Yucca treculeana, *growing in the Chihuahuan Desert.*

Hedgehog cactus, Echinocereus polyacanthus, *of the Chihuahuan Desert.*

Flowering Thelocactus bicolor *in the Chihuahuan. All photos this page and opposite, courtesy of the Desert Botanical Garden.*

the Chihuahuan. Mule deer, ocelots, rabbits, javelina, bobcats, and again the reptiles make their life here.

Big Bend National Park, situated on the Texas-Mexico border, and the Guadalupe Mountains National Park provide camping areas and hiking trails to acquaint the foot explorer with the Chihuahuan Desert.

Painted Desert

Rainbows of color and form make the Painted Desert one of the most tourist-traveled areas in the American Southwest. It is a flat, broad land surrounded by low mountains and flat-topped mesas rising above the desert floor. Great canyons and cliffs display subtle pastel colors, brought out again in the painted sands and petrified wood.

Since most of this desert is above 3,500 feet, winters can be cold and snowy. Summers are hot, with intense thunder-storms, high clouds, and clear atmosphere. (This is being changed with the coal deposit exploitation in the Four Corners area.) Much of the desert floor is barren and wind-swept sand or rock, while in other places it is covered with low scrub, yucca, sagebrush, and many grasses. At the sou-theast end is Petrified Forest National Park in which 150-million-year-old tree trunks can be seen. Canyon de Chelly, Monument Valley, Rainbow Bridge, Sunset Crater, and many Indian ruins are located in this desert. It is the homeland of the Navajo and Hopi Indian tribes. The Little Colorado River, which drains this desert plateau, runs northwest through the barren land into the main Colorado River, cutting gorges as deep as 3,000 feet. An artist's palette of changing colors and land forms, this sculptured plateau is awesomely silent, broken now and then by fierce gusts of wind and thunderstorms. Monument Valley, an area of singular beauty, is a huge temple to the gods of wind and water, a constantly changing light show of cloud, sky, butte, and shadow.

Dinosaurs, amphibians, and reptiles once lived here in a world of tree ferns and tall pines. Today, yuccas, cacti, and grasses provide the environment for coyote, bobcat, fox, rabbit, and numerous rodents. The beautiful desert rattlesnake makes his home here, his pink to reddish brown body blending into the landscape.

Colorado Desert

The Colorado Desert is the hottest spot in the United States. Most of the terrain is close to sea level and can become an oven with daily summer temperatures climbing to 120 degrees Fahrenheit in the shade. Hikers should avoid daytime summer exposure. Early mornings and evenings are possible hiking times, but even then the heat can climb to more than 100 degrees. Average rainfall varies from a trace to five inches.

Bear grass, Nolina bigelovii, *growing in the Colorado Desert. Courtesy of the Desert Botanical Gardens.*

If enough moisture falls in the winter, the desert floor is transformed into a carpet of pink sand verbena and white desert primrose. Ocotillos put out their clusters of orange-red blossoms. An exclusive inhabitant of the Colorado Desert is the ghostly smoke tree, made up of silvery grey-green branches that look like the remnants of a desert campfire. Mesquite, catclaw, ironwood, and desert willow live in the dry streambeds. Fan palms provide shade for the exceptional oases found in the surrounding mountain canyons. These oases attract all kinds of desert wildlife at night—bobcats, coyotes, foxes, mule deer, raccoons. The desert bighorn sheep dwells in the rugged mountains.

Now your appetite is whetted for more information. You are anxious to experience the desert and its many moods first-hand. Great, but let's make a plan to take advantage of all that the lands of little water have to offer. We need to . . .

2

Plan Ahead

. . . I thought you brought the water.

"Hey Dave, reach into your pack and bust out the brandy.
We've been a week on this climb and we need a break."

"Uh, we left it at our last camp."

"Oh no! I'll settle for some of the wine then."

"Uh, remember? We dropped that off up at camp 3."

"Great! And I suppose we left the toilet paper up there
too."

"Nope. We left that at base camp."

"Great planning!"

Kes Teter, Mt. McKinley, Alaska,
June, 1971

There is an old army saying called the Five Ps: Prior
Planning Prevents Poor Performance. How true. Prior planning for hiking and backpacking means knowing where you
are on the ground and on a map at all times; having adequate
food and water; knowing about when you will arrive at your
destination; being aware of the natural history of the environment; being able to handle rain, snow, sleet, and hail as
well as 120° heat; and knowing what to do in an emergency.

19

If you have planned for these, you will find yourself free to enjoy the total experience—the sights, sounds, smells, and feels of the natural environment which supported early man for hundreds of thousands of years. Your wilderness senses will be reawakened and you will slowly become one with the desert— its creatures, its plants, its canyons and mesas, its ever-changing sun-shadow light.

The way to be prepared is to allow enough *time* to make all the necessary plans before you venture out. Some of you are just starting out and looking forward to your first hike. Others of you have been taking day hikes and want to start going overnight, a whole new ball game. Some of you have gone on weekend backpacks and now want to try an extended cross-country trip into unknown territory. And, there are probably thousands of hikers and backpackers who have been camping in the wilderness for years without practicing camping conservation and leave-no-trace ethics. Granted, it is difficult to slow down to the desert's pace on a two-day weekend after five hectic days running the race of the rats. But it's worth a try. When you have slowed down enough to start tasting that fresh rainwater collected in the rock pocket, to smell that dry sandstone or wet creosote bush, to feel the texture of sand verbena and horned toad, to get up and watch the dawn display—when you have planned enough time to control your trip from start to finish with enough minutes and hours left to just gaze around and drink in the clear desert air, then you will feel surrounded by the wonder and discovery that lies waiting.

Okay, that all sounds good. But how do you make these plans to get the most enjoyment out of the time you have? Do you want to go from point A to point B just to say you've done it? Do you want to escape from civilization into a primitive environment? Do you want to study geology and landforms, animal life, plant life? To capture the desert on film? To have a coming-together family experience? Or maybe to step up to the summit of some lonely, craggy desert peak? For most folks, it's probably a combination of these. But whatever the reasons, the same principles of planning apply.

Route Plan

If you already have a destination picked out, good. If not, then you might start with the recommended reading in the

A good place to start is with a visit to a park or monument in the desert area most interesting to you. These usually have excellent trail maps, guides, and up-to-date information about the wildlife, natural history, and hiking needs.

Appendix. I have starred the books I think most important; I suggest you read the others at your leisure. Another good place to start is with a visit to a park or monument in the desert area most interesting to you. These usually offer excellent trail maps, guides, and up-to-date information about wildlife, natural history, and hiking needs.

All right, you want to plan a trip on your own. You have a general idea of the climate, geography, flora and fauna, and you want to get out among 'em. Start with U.S. Geological Survey topographic maps of the specific areas you have in

Sometimes a Lower Sonoran Husky can help find lost or overgrown trails. Be sure to carry a comb and heavy-duty tweezers for the unavoidable cholla cactus in the paw. Photo by Dave Ganci.

mind. They can be obtained by writing to the federal government offices listed in the Appendix. You can also find them at your local backpacking and blueprint shops.

How do you know which maps to buy? First you get a map index of the state you wish to explore. This should be available from a local shop. Match the index to a good state road map. The index will tell you which topographic quadrangle to get to cover the specific areas of interest to you. The most popular maps are the 7½-minute and 15-minute sizes, which cover approximately 62 square miles and 248 square miles respectively.

It's fun to learn to read these maps. Ask the government office or your local shop for a map symbol pamphlet. Learn how to read contour lines and terrain features. (We'll talk a little more about this later.) If you want to become an expert on map reading, look in the geography section of your library for a book on map interpretation. You will learn how to tell what kind of vegetation grows there, what crops are most important, what people do for a living, what type of climate and landforms exist, how much rainfall the area gets, where power lines, roads, and trails (don't rely on these) are located, and many other items of information that will assist you in your planning.

You've got some maps now of a place you want to explore. You have an abandoned mine shaft as your destination, or maybe a desert spring or creek, or a mesa top, or a mountain summit, or maybe just a round trip hike to enjoy the desert scenery. With maps spread out, you now are ready to make your time and distance plan.

Time and Distance Plan

If you are planning a one-day hike, everything is pretty simple. All you need is a small pack, the right clothing, some food, plenty of water, camera, hat, flashlight, foam pad for afternoon snoozes, and a can of beer to cool off in a cold desert spring (if you can find one). And don't forget the maps. If it's to be an overnight camp, you are in a different league. You will need sleeping gear, more food, possibly cooking utensils, and maybe a shelter plus a few more personal items. But whether you are going out for a day or a week you still need a time and distance plan.

First, figure out how many hours you want to travel each day. Then determine how many miles you can cover on your route in each day's time. You should set up a campsite at least a couple hours before sunset so you don't have to rush dinner, and so you can lie back on your air mattress and take in the sunset. This is the time that the day and night shifts of the animal world are changing. Night creatures are getting ready for the hunt and day creatures are heading for a snooze.

The distance you can travel in one day is determined by the terrain, the elevation gain, whether you'll follow a trail or go cross-country, the condition of the group, the weight you are carrying, and the pace you want to set. Use the topographical map to visualize the entire trip from start to finish. If you are carrying a light day pack, you can average about three miles an hour over easy terrain. Put twenty or thirty pounds in it and you slow down. Heavier than that and you may make two miles an hour. Over tough terrain you may make anywhere from one mile to half a mile an hour.

The map's contour lines and other symbols will give you a picture of the ground you will be hiking over. Use the scale at the bottom of the map and measure off a string equal to a mile. Measure the route with the string to get how many straight miles you have figured you can cover for the day. Now look at the elevation gains and losses. Figure the distance on steep ascents and descents. Cross-country routes may take you twice as long as on trail. If you figure you can average two miles an hour, multiply that by how many hours you want to be on the move and you will get approximately how many miles you will be able to cover that day. Mark that spot on the map. You should plan to camp somewhere close to that mark. Look for level spots and water sources close to that mark. Choose a spot, circle it, and then go over your route with an orange or yellow felt-tip pen to make it easy to follow when you're out in the field. In a later chapter you will learn how to spot yourself on the map at all times during

K & R pedometer. Footsteps along the trail are measured as mileage on the pedometer. Courtesy of Precise International.

Take a look at your route and try to visualize the different terrain features that your contour lines designate. Make mental note of the high points, cliffs, dry and intermittent streambeds, trails, and other man-made features.

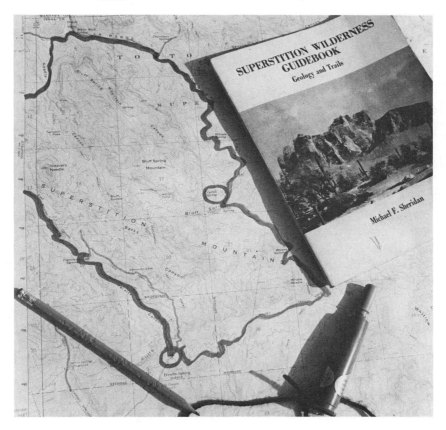

your hike, and therefore, keep track of your time and distance as you go along. But for now, take a look at your route and try to visualize the different terrain features that the contour lines designate. Make a mental note of the high points, cliffs, valleys, dry and intermittent streambeds, trails, and other man-made features.

What about a compass? A compass should not be a substitute for your senses and brainpower. It is only an adjunct when you don't have enough information otherwise. If you learn to use time, distance, and terrain features, you will seldom need a compass. As you gain experience, you will leave your watch in the pack also because you will become aware of the sun's movements and its relation to the time of day.

Everything's looking good with your daily time and distance plan. It's time to think of the weather.

Climate Plan

Desert climate is fairly predictable due to the predominant high pressure systems that allow the sun to do its job so well. Depending on the area, winter and summer storms follow fairly predictable patterns in the desert. You should always check with the local weather forecaster to get predicted highs and lows. These are the extremes that you must protect against. Remember, official air temperature is measured in a shady box with no reflective heat. Real desert heat includes direct sun and reflection off the ground which can add from five to forty degrees to the reading.

Summer desert thunderstorms are unmatched in their dra-

(Opposite page) A typical dry, mild winter day hike in the Sonoran Desert.
(Below) A not-so-typical day on the same desert during a winter storm. Photos by Dave Ganci.

matic displays of thunder, lightning, and clouds. They usually build up during the day, then dump in the afternoon with great flash, bang, and dust. They can dissipate their energy in a short period of time, sending thundering heads of water down usually dry desert streambeds, turning them into temporary avenues of destruction. Don't set up camp in washes—period. Summer showers can be very refreshing and cooling. They usually pass quickly, and everything dries just as quickly. When I get caught in a summer storm, I usually stand out in it and get soaking wet. This keeps me cool for at least an hour afterwards.

If you are planning a trip during the summer months, you can beat the heat by hiking during the early mornings and late afternoons, setting up some shade and taking a midday siesta just as most of the wildlife does.

You've spent an hour or so with your maps, desert wildlife books, and plans. Now it's a good time to think about getting some exercise.

Do Some Running

Of course the better your physical condition, the better prepared you will be to handle the rigors of hiking and backpacking. A leisurely day hike is not rigorous, and anyone should be able to handle this enjoyable type of sojourn. Long day hikes and overnights usually demand a great deal more effort from the body, so conditioning is valuable. Jogging, climbing stairs and hills, mountain running, and jumping rope are all good cardiovascular-building exercises. I am used to getting up at 5 A.M. and running five miles (well, not every morning). You can bet, however, that I started out with one mile and worked up to it. This forces me to get to bed earlier and drastically cuts down my nightlife. A side benefit from all this is supposed to be a prolonged life span. Hmmm? Well, anyway, it makes the day longer.

A "plan ahead" story comes to mind when I think of my first-altitude climbing experience in the Andes Mountains of Peru. It was during my "wander years," 1959-60, and I found myself in Lima, Peru. I hung around a well-known hotel where mountaineers from all over the world gathered before heading up into the Cordillera Blanca—the popular ice and snow range of the Andes. I met up with an American group and joined their team. I had no equipment. I borrowed a sleeping bag from one person, heavy jacket from another, bought pants, gloves, shirts, and other clothing from a surplus store. I bought a pair of climbing boots from a German alpinist who was on his way back home. I topped all this well-planned paraphernalia off with a straw hat that I actually wore to the summit of a 20,000-foot peak. I would plan differently next time.

You've just come back from jogging, your calves are tied up in knots, and you are finishing off the cold orange juice. You go back to the maps and look again at that Jeep trail that leads you to the hiking trailhead, but you don't have a Jeep! You had better start thinking about a . . .

3

Desert Vehicle Plan

. . . You mean the spare is flat, too?

Your wilderness travel actually starts when the tires of your vehicle leave the highway and turn onto that sometimes-maintained dirt road with the signs that seem to disappear or point in the wrong direction or are full of bullet holes. The desert vehicle plan includes adequate road study on both highway and topographical maps to keep you headed in the right direction. Remember, man-made features change quite often, whereas topographic features are 99 percent constant. This means that a road or turn shown on a topographical map dated 1953 may have changed dramatically. Get the most up-to-date local road map you can find. Check such sources as the American Automobile Association, U.S. Forest Service, U.S. Bureau of Land Management, and U.S. Park Service. Talk to people who live or work near the area where you wish to travel. Service station attendants, café people, and motel people can be helpful. You can also end up with more answers than you want, but you may also get some tidbits of useful information such as "Don't cross that streambed in July or August because you may not get back across until October."

Check mileage as you go, and compare this to the time-

distance plan you have drawn out on your map. Keep track of topographic features such as mountains, creeks, cliffs, and riverbeds as you go. Know where you are on the map at all times! The trailhead may be close to the highway, in which case you have little worry. Then again, it may be many twisting, turning, flat miles over relatively featureless desert sand. You have to keep track of your direction and progress in case you want to get back and suddenly everything looks the same—or different.

Time and distance can be distorted on open deserts due to tricks the eyes play on you in the dry, clear air, and due to the distance between prominent landmarks on the terrain. This lack of clutter in the landscape normally should make deter-

(Above) Keep ahead of the hood. Check your mileage, location, and destination. A Maricopa County Ranger helps a hiker locate his position in the White Tanks County Park. Courtesy of Maricopa County Parks, Arizona.

(Left) Use landmarks and maps to keep track of your location. Photo by Dave Ganci.

mination of location easy, but the eye makes distant features seem closer than they actually are. I have stood on the edge of the Grand Canyon many times looking way across at distant temples, only to realize my eyes were bringing them closer just as a zoom lens would. Because of this, in my early canyon treks I misjudged the time required to reach my objectives. Light and shadow also play many mind tricks in open desert areas. Features will look much different in the morning than they do in the afternoon.

Assign at least one passenger to act as navigator to keep you on your course. The driver will probably be busy enough avoiding rocks and gullies. The navigator should mark features not shown on the map, landmarks like stock tanks, windmills, and new buildings since the maps came out. Make notes on the map of road signs you find. Write down odometer readings at turns and Ys in the road. Get out and pile up some stones at intersections you are in doubt about so you will recognize them on the return trip.

Perhaps it seems I am overemphasizing the use of maps, but I don't think so. They are your guides, your insurance, your peace of mind. If you always know where you are, you cannot get lost. On the return trip to the highway, you will have a detailed plan already worked out. Then the next trip into the same place will be a snap. You would also be wise to leave a copy of your map with the proposed route, destination, and estimated time of return with a relative or friend. If you have not notified that person of your whereabouts within twenty-four hours after your expected time of return, he will know that he should initiate a search.

Vehicle Survival

You will need some extra gear to allow your buggy to negotiate the challenges and hazards of backcountry driving. You may be a long way from home when the water hose breaks. Here are some of the items to consider carrying along.

extra water hose
2 mounted spare tires filled to correct capacity
1 large heavy-duty bumper jack and 1 hydraulic axle jack
jumper cables
extra fan belt
tool box
extra battery fully charged
at least 5 gallons of extra gas
4-lug crossbar tire iron
1 week's supply of survival rations
1 sparkplug type tire pump
2 plywood jack pads about 1 foot square
4 pieces of old carpet each at least 1 foot wide by 4 feet long, for use
    if car gets stuck
assortment of nuts and bolts
1 long-handled shovel

electric repair tape
2 tarps for laying on the ground if you must crawl under to try to
    dislodge broken tail pipe
extra wire to rig the tail pipe back in place
1 small fire extinguisher
heavy-duty work gloves
1 axe
tow chain or nylon tow rope
hose clamps
marine repair tape
heavy-duty light source in addition to 2 small flashlights
gasket material
signal mirror
5 quarts extra oil
extra brake fluid
rubber washers of all sizes
AT LEAST 10 GALLONS OF WATER

Statistics show that about half of all highway tow truck assists are due to battery or electrical problems. Bad tires take another big percentage. The following is a list of some of the other more common problems of desert driving.

overheated engine
damaged tie-rods
getting stuck in sand or washes
running out of gas (believe it or not)
punctured fuel tank
hole in oil pan due to high centering
broken oil line
vapor lock
cooling system problems

The major causes of these and other desert driving pains are speed and carelessness. That's why you would be in better shape if you knew a bit about desert truckin'.

Desert Truckin'
A backcountry road is to your car what the wilderness is to you: a new, different, more challenging, and demanding

environment. A truck or jeep is, of course, partially attuned to this off-highway stuff, but a low slung passenger car could be in for some trouble. The same principle of planning enough time so you don't have to hurry applies to desert driving as well as desert hiking. Drive slowly and enjoy the scenery. Don't forget to give everything a last minute check at the filling station before you take off. Check all tires including spares; check oil, water, and batteries. Make sure your water containers are full. Top off the fuel and check the 5-gallon gas tank.

Here are a few time-tested backcountry driving techniques. (1) Take two vehicles in case one breaks down. (2) Turning around on narrow roads with sand shoulders should be done with a companion clearing the tires from outside the vehicle. Keep the back tires on solid ground even if it takes a half hour to turn around. (3) Drive very slowly over rocky roads. Rocks are death to marginal tires. (4) Sand tires are advisable for soft sandy roads. You can deflate your tires in a pinch, but make sure you can inflate them again. (5) Learn techniques of vehicle extraction and field maintenance. See the Appendix for reference to an excellent pamphlet by Alan H. Siebert.

Help

In the unlikely event that you get stranded for whatever reason and cannot extricate yourself, here are some courses of action.

Sit down and make an estimate of the situation. You should know just about where you are on the map. Is it better to wait at the vehicle or to try to travel on foot for assistance? Since you have left a copy of your route with a friend or relative, you will have until twenty-four hours after your estimated time of arrival before anyone is going to look for you. How long is that from the time you broke down? How far are you from any sign of ranch life or the highway or a gas station? Do you have enough water to stay put until help arrives? What about the other people in your party? Are they prepared to make a long hike out? They should be if you had planned a backpack trip. If you were prepared for a day hike or car camp you may opt for staying with the vehicle. Do you have flares, smoke bombs, or banners?

Every situation varies. That is why you must first sit down and write out the various factors and options. If you decide to head back to civilization alone, leaving the others at the vehicle, you must make sure that they will stay by the vehicle until help arrives. You may elect to take everyone with you. With your map you should have no trouble retracing your route to the various landmarks and signposts. You can average about three miles an hour on flat terrain. You must make a water plan for the walk back. Take twice as much as the plan calls for. One gallon for every fifteen miles is a good average. If you figure you will be longer than a day hiking out, do your walking in the early morning from about 6 A.M. to 10 A.M. Rest in shade until around 4 P.M., then go on for another four hours. You may have to make camp in the dark, but covering distance is essential in this situation.

If you elect to stay at the vehicle, set up plenty of shade with tarps. Pull everything out of the vehicle, including seats, and make a layer of insulation between people and ground. Drape "help" banners over the hood and have flares and smoke bombs ready in case low-flying aircraft wander over the area. Don't use them all; save some for the official search that will be conducted when you have been reported missing. Stay in the shade all day. Now is the time to catch up on your reading.

Back in the old days, my buddy Barry Whitlock and I used to go out snake and rabbit hunting at night. Barry was an amateur herpetologist, and I was an amateur Jeep driver. One night we were headlighting a desert jackrabbit across the open desert north of Phoenix in my four-wheel-drive pickup. We skirted around a huge mound, and all of a sudden the ground seemed to get mushy. It didn't look any different than any of the rest of the earth. We started sliding around, and the pickup started tilting to the right.

"What's going on?" I hollered.

"Beats the heck out of me," Barry answered.

We listed to a 45-degree angle and were stuck. The right side of the Jeep was buried up to the door panel. We jumped out and took a close look at the ground. It was muddy underneath the surface layer on the right side. We both scratched out heads. Where did the water come from? Then we remembered the mound. It was a built-up cattle watering tank, and it had leaked out around the mound, but was not visible on the surface. We had gone off the edge on the right side, but had two good wheels on solid ground. Well, we dug and filled it, put into four-wheel backward and forward, rocked, pushed, kicked, screamed, hollered, and moved forward about a foot.

We succeeded in burying the Jeep deeper. It was a long walk back to Shea Boulevard where we sat in front of a bar and smoked until we got a ride into town.

Off-Road Vehicles

I used to tear around the desert in a four-wheeler and a motorcycle. Not anymore. Times have changed. I have changed. There is no place for off-road desert destruction now. Recent research undertaken by the U.S. Fish and Wildlife Service on the California desert has shown that off-road vehicle impact has resulted in the killing and maiming of ground-dwelling animals, the crushing of ground nests and burrows, the disappearance of bird life, the destruction of vegetation and soil-supporting root structures; the reduction of annual spring wild flower growth, and the general disruption of wildlife habitat. Here is a statement from the Bureau of Interior Wildlife Research Report 8:

"The present study provides evidence that ORVs detrimentally affect desert wildlife and creosote shrub habitat. The ORVs have been extensively used for less than a decade in the Mohave Desert, but already there has been widespread negative impact on desert communities. The available data indicate that continued intensive ORV activities will be increasingly detrimental to the wildlife resources of the California Desert. The impact of these ORV activities must be recognized in present and future management programs so as to minimize or curtail losses of irreplaceable habitat and associated wildlife living on Natural Resources Land, State, military, and private holdings."

Off-road vehicles have provided access to prehistoric ruins, burial grounds, archaeological and paleontological sites, human inscription sites and other historically significant areas. These areas have in turn been vandalized, shot up with firearms, looted, burned, and treated with little respect for their historic value. Granted, only a small minority of non-thinking people do these things. And the lack of consideration is not limited to ORV users. There are backpackers and hikers who are just as destructive. The only difference is that the ORV allows the destructive person to do more harm, more quickly.

I am not personally condemning ORV users. I used to be one. I hope to get them thinking about the long-range effects of their hobbies and to convince them to stick to roads and jeep trails. It took millions of years of evolution and adaptation to produce the deserts we have. It won't take long to destroy them. Then it will take many years to re-establish them, if that is possible. A responsible attitude takes this into consideration.

Well, now that you have decided to put a set of tires on your desert driving vehicle and have picked up the necessary tools and survival gear, your machine will be all dressed and ready to go. But *you're* not dressed and ready to go. You need to be thinking about a . . .

4

Desert Dress and Paraphernalia Plan

. . . Do you think we should bring an umbrella?

"So I produced a traveling-bag and placed therein the following articles:—a 'diamond edition' of Longfellow, the Harper's text of Horace, a manifold note-book for the *res gestae*, a change of flannel, a tooth-brush, my sister's spool of snuff-colored thread, and my mother's hussif. This latter article was very wonderfully and inscrutably made, and contained a thimble, an elegant assortment of pins, needles and buttons, scissors, and leaves for needles, some of white flannel, daintily stitched with pink thread around the edges, and some of scarlet, switched with white. When wrapped together it was no larger than a cylindrical nutmeg-grater; and it was of such marvelous potency in repairing rips and rents, that I herewith state my belief that, if my mother simply sat in the room with it, it could keep house itself.

"I was dressed in a pair of doeskin trowsers; light top-boots, with the ends of the trowsers inserted therein; a shortish frock-coat; and a planter's hat.

"Thus rigged out, and equipped with a mighty jackknife, I left Raleigh on New Year's day, 1868."*

---

*Powers, *Afoot and Alone: A Walk from Sea to Sea by the Southern Route*, p. 19.

My qualifications for discussing the various desert dress and paraphernalia options come from eight years in the retailing of backpacking merchandise and twenty-three years of tramping. As general manager of the Camp Trails retail stores—called High Adventure Headquarters (now called Holubar Mountaineering) in Phoenix, Arizona—from 1969 to 1975, I saw a tremendous parade of backpacking, mountaineering, and ski-touring merchandise pass in review. I was involved in production, research and development, and advertising with Camp Trails. I have worn at least one pair of most major brands of hiking boots. I've slept in various configurations of goose down, synthetic, duck down, and foam bags. Under them I've put air mattresses, foam pads, various styles of ensolite, climbing ropes, and bare ground (not recommended). My first pack was an old army A-frame, but I've gone through various makes and models of bag-and-frame combinations into the newer, stylish internal-frame models. I've slept, (part of the time) in tents on Mount McKinley that I thought for sure were going to blow us all away and back down to Anchorage. On the desert, I've tried tarps, tube tents, mosquito-net-lined tents, full-wall tents, and my favorite, no tent at all. I've put matches to stoves using white gas, kerosene, butane, propane, alcohol, and gasoline.

One of my policies at High Adventure was to field test all new merchandise sold in the shop so that we would have firsthand information to relate to customers. Either I or one of my employees used the item and provided a written report on its function. Clothing, knives, survival gear, backpack foods, climbing hardware—all were tested. I have talked with all kinds of hikers and backpackers regarding their favorite paraphernalia.

With this background I can safely make one definite statement about paraphernalia: Nobody knows what is best for someone else. I can only suggest what to start with if you have not already purchased gear. You will have to make the ultimate decisions about gear based on what you read, what you hear, and what you think your needs will be. You will know much more after your first trip or two. Therefore, my first suggestion is to start simple and cheap. Buying gear wisely is like learning to play poker. Don't raise the bid too high until you have a grip on the game. Sit down and make a list of the gear you want to start with. Figure how much money you can afford to spend on this equipment. Then visit your local camping or hiking shop. The shop should have catalogs or information sheets on most of the products it sells. If printed sales literature isn't on hand, ask the owner to get some for you. When you have looked over the merchandise, ask to talk to the salesperson who knows the most about backpack gear.

Arrives the expert.

Tell him or her what your needs are and what you plan on doing. You can tell pretty quickly if the individual wants to listen to your needs or if he wants to tell you how expert he is. You can also tell quickly if the salesperson is more interested in selling you something rather than in filling your needs. Listen to his pitch and ask all the questions that come to mind. Don't make a buying decision impulsively. Tell him "thank you," and take the catalogs home. They are fun to look over; the exercise feels like making out a list for Santa. You will see pretty models, tightly stuffed packs, puffed up sleeping bags, and perfectly pitched tents. There is usually a great deal of technical and nice-to-know information in these catalogs, too.

In your overall dress and paraphernalia plan, leave room for considering the commercial sewing kits on the market. They offer a tremendous variety of clothing and gear for the do-it-yourself-minded outdoors person. They constitute a money-saving, if not time-saving, alternative to the completed object. Make sure you check sewing instructions from the various manufacturers so that you will not bite off more than you can sew. Some backpacking shops offer seminars and classes on sewing kits. Holubar, Frostline, and Altra Kits offer programs through school home economics classes.

The rest of this chapter will point out some of the factors to keep in mind when you shop the stores and catalogs for desert hiking gear. My last word of advice on the general subject of

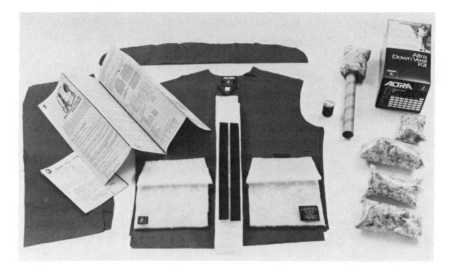

(Above) A vest kit for beginners who want to make their own gear. Courtesy of Altra, Inc.

desert dress and paraphernalia is to be realistic about what you really need. Although I recommend that you plan your trip thoroughly, I do not believe you should wrap yourself up in a protective bubble of plastic or nylon to insulate yourself from *all* the elements *all* the time. You might as well stay home and read adventure stories if you have no desire to feel the seasons. That has to be one of the reasons you go out in the wilderness—to let your body exhilarate with its own protective mechanisms. Feel a little wind! Get a little chilly! Soak up a little rain! Sweat a little! Not too much, mind you, just enough to feel the reawakening of all your senses. There is something very soul-satisfying about taking your shirt off briefly in a strong, blowing rain and feeling your body respond to those cold, wet, stinging drops. You want to scream to the heavens, "Yes, by God, I am alive!"

Patagonia shelled Synchilla jacket is ideal for the mild desert winters. Photo by Aimee Madsen, courtesy of Patagonia.

Hats

The old saying, "If your feet are cold, put your hat on," is true. The head surface loses a tremendous amount of heat in cold weather and absorbs a tremendous amount of heat in hot weather. You need a hat that has at least a 2½-inch brim and a crown that is higher than your head. It should also be flexible and well ventilated with holes. It must be made of indestructible material like felt. There is no other item of equipment except boots that gets treated with as much abuse. Yet I don't believe there is another item of clothing that expresses individuality more than a hat. Ask any cowboy.

Shop the surplus and secondhand stores. You'll find hats by the hundreds. But don't buy a straw hat. A straw hat provides good shade and ventilation but it is definitely destructible. You can easily end up with a few handfuls of broken straw after you have rolled over on it, stepped on it, or laid a pack on it. If the hat you choose doesn't have good ventilation, cut extra holes in the crown. Fasten a chin strap to your hat to hold it on in the wind. Desert dust devils love to snatch hats from your head, zoom them up to unbelievable heights, then send them floating into the next canyon. Mesquite and catclaw will snatch them away also. Testimony to all this is that I have found more hats on the desert than I have bought. Hats are great for doffing to hikers of the opposite sex, too!

The Fjord wool pullover hat for those chilly evenings or northern desert days. Courtesy of Wigwam Mills, Inc.

What about those cool desert evenings? You should carry a knitted pullover cap or balaclava. You can wear one under your ventilated hat and be ready for the worst of both worlds.

A large bandana serves a multitude of purposes. You can soak it at the water hole and tie it around your head for evaporative cooling. It serves as a sweatband, a neck protector, and a washcloth. In an emergency you can even use it to blow your nose.

Sunglasses

Sunglasses are a very personal item, but very handy in the glare of morning and afternoon sun. Reflective light from bright sand and dust can be almost as blinding as from snow. Polarized lenses are nice. They cut down reflection. I don't buy expensive sunglasses because I have broken them in every possible way. Get an elastic strap to keep the glasses on during rapid head movement, especially when your face is slippery with perspiration. This way you can hang them around your neck when you don't need them. You can also use them when you lie back by that desert spring, face the sun, and start picking up a tan.

Suntan and Skin Protectors

Unless your doctor advises against it, try to get at least a moderate suntan before rambling in the desert. Even then, take a sun-screening agent along with you. The laws of physics state that you will conserve water if you don't expose your skin to the sun. However, we are not on a survival mission here, so suit yourself. I do a lot of shirtless hiking because I like to feel the radiant warmth of the sun and the cooling effect of desert breezes. But make no mistake about it; don't get overexposed. If you have not pretanned your extremities, keep your shirt on. There are various lotions, creams, blocking agents, salves, and ointments on the market. Ask your doctor and check drug stores as well as camping stores. If you have a receding hairline, be doubly careful. I know of a couple people who suffered sunburned crowns, and it had to be as miserable as blistered feet.

Carry a lip-protecting agent such as Chapstick or other fruity-flavored concoction. Lipstick may be the answer for women. There is nothing that will stop a smile faster than dry, cracked lips.

Carry a small plastic bottle of plain hand lotion. Use it in the mornings and evenings, before and after cooking. Your hands will dry out in desert air. They can then start cracking and give you those little infuriating fingertip skin breaks called "the splits." Hand lotion can prevent these.

"It is not often that you meet the right and necessary combination of weather and privacy so that you can carry the keep-adjusting-your-clothing-all-day-long system to its logical conclusion. The first time I did so for any length of time was on my long Grand Canyon journey. Of course, I exercised due care for a few days with the previously shielded sector of my anatomy. In particular, I pressed the bandana into service as a fig leaf. But soon I was walking almost all day long with nothing above my ankles except a hat."*

Shirts

You probably have some old cotton work shirts stuffed in a closet. Or, again, shop the surplus stores. Don't get synthetic material; it does not breathe. Buy larger sizes than you normally wear for freer movement and air circulation. Get button-up, not pullover styles for ventilation control. Get collars for neck protection. I personally like short sleeves because of the ventilation, but I also take a long-sleeved shirt for protection against the catclaws and underbrush. Shirts for hiking should also have big pockets to stash things in and extra-long tails that stay tucked in when you bend, squat, or reach for those early summer mesquite beans. If you can't find a shirt that already has these features, sew them on yourself. Light colors are best for reflecting and bright colors are best for photographs. For cooler weather or cold evenings, take along a mediumweight wool shirt, also with long tail.

Sweaters and Jackets

A lightweight goose or duck down, or synthetic-filled jacket is a good all-round cool-weather garment. A vest with a heavy wool shirt underneath serves the same purpose. Synthetic fills

---

*Fletcher, Colin. *The New Complete Walker*, p. 311. New York, Alfred A. Knopf, 1974.

A light goose or duck down, or synthetic-filled vest is a good all-round cool temperature garment. A vest with a heavy wool shirt underneath serves the same purpose. Courtesy of The North Face.

hold up better than natural fills in wet weather, but that is seldom a problem in the desert. Now, if you go up into the mountain islands that sprout from the desert floor, you will need more clothing. Mountain weather might convince you to buy a heavier jacket.

Of course, there will always be the exception in weather conditions, the freak Pacific Northwest storm that drops down into the Lower Sonoran for a day to wreak havoc on unsuspecting desert hikers who are lounging around at camp in the Superstitions in their shorts and T-shirts. But that is part of the game, and it keeps things interesting.

Pants

Shorts or long pants? I usually take both. And they are both about two sizes bigger than I normally wear, for ease of movement and ventilation. If the terrain permits, and I have prepared my skin to resist sunburn, I like to hike in shorts. Almost all the desert hikers I know do the same. I also carry long pants for brush country and cooler evenings.

Experiment! Life or death won't hang on the loose thread of a pair of baggy corduroy shorts, or whipcord shorts, or heavy cotton duck shorts. All are good, sturdy materials. Beware of the close-fitting, fashionable, chic, "outdoor" look becoming available in department and specialty stores. The glamour magazines are getting with the great outdoors, and you will probably see the hip, beautifully groomed, and lipsticked fashion models decked out in the latest safari pants, pointing a finger toward the next page with the same model displaying the "peasant" look.

You want loose-fitting comfort—baggy if you will—and durability, with lots of pockets. You can always sew them on with big buttons and butterflies. The old army surplus combat pants with cargo pockets were ideal, but are hard to find nowadays.

In extra-hot weather, I sometimes hike with my fly unbuttoned and without undershorts. I haven't been arrested yet for indecent exposure. I usually button up, though, when afternoon Lower Sonoran thunderstorms really break loose and dump rain on me.

Rain Gear

A lot of desert hikers welcome the chance to get wet because it is a cool and refreshing change after hours or days of dry heat. In the Arizona desert thunderstorms are a happening. In Phoenix we sometimes climb up on our roofs to watch the thunder and lightning fireworks.

Most summer storms are short and not-so-sweet. They can be awesome displays of power that put our technologies into proper perspective. They usually pass quickly and leave little behind to show for their fury except the dry washes and arroyos that have suddenly become torrents of fast-moving water. But they dry up soon; by the next morning everything looks the same. The dry earth has soaked up the moisture in a race with the sun that is trying to evaporate it. Fresh desert smells linger for a day or two, and then blossoms begin to sprout as carpets of wild flowers spread across the brown landscape. They too complete their life cycle in a few days or weeks, set seed, then curl up and die back into the soil.

I usually carry a poncho on a desert hike because it has so many uses. I can use it for any number of shelter types, water cachements, and rain protection. In the Lower Sonoran Desert, if the rain is a typical short-term outburst, I enjoy hiking in it and usually get wet from head to foot. As long as there is an hour or two of daylight left after the shower stops, the dry desert air will cool me off and get me dry by dinner. My boots will usually dry out on the next day's hike.

For longer, winter storms and in the higher deserts, you may need a good tent, rain parka or rain pants. This consideration should be part of your climate control plan.

Desert dust storms are more frequent than rainstorms. We have sat atop Squaw Peak in Phoenix, watching the miles-long, hundreds-of-feet-high fronts rolling in from the east over the valley. We have laughed at the unwary souls down on the golf course or tennis court, who don't see the storm coming until it is too late, only to remember that we have forgotten to close our house and car windows. Many times these rolling dust storms intermingle with the rain to create a third kind of storm: the mud storm. Large brown drops splatter everything with a light brown pattern that turns into free-form art when it dries. Now, whenever a thunderstorm blows into the Phoenix area, and we don't happen to be out in the desert, we throw some cheese, bread, salami, and wine into a day pack and head up to our local training mountain, Squaw Peak. We find a niche near the summit, snuggle in, and watch the show.

In the summer of 1970, Kes Teter, Charlie Rigden, Glenn Kappel, and I were on a ten-day drink-beer-and-climb trip to the Pacific Northwest, where our summit goals were Mt. Shasta, California; Mt. Hood, Oregon; and Mt. Rainier in the state of Washington. We got all decked out in our ice and snow mountain parkas, wind pants, mountain boots, ropes, and ice axes, and we were hoofing it through the snow up to Camp Muir, the overnight hut on the way to the summit of Mt. Rainier. We would spend the night there, climb to the top the next morning, and descend back down to Paradise Lodge in the afternoon. We arrived at Muir on the afternoon of the first day and, along with several other climbers, were enjoying a little afternoon wine inside the hut. We heard a commotion outside. Upon investigation, we found some climbers gathered round an elderly gentleman nattily attired in dress shirt, tie, vest, street shoes, country hat, and big smile. Seems he just came up for the afternoon. We approached him.

"Do you always dress like that to climb Mt. Rainier?" we asked.

"Oh, I'm not going to the summit," he replied, "I used to climb Rainier all the time in my youth, but now I just come up to Muir to enjoy the scenery."

He walked around awhile, then bid us good day and disappeared into the mist on his way back down to the lodge.

"From the days of iron men and wooden ships," we all laughed.

I don't advise beginners to wear dress shoes on Mt. Rainier or in the desert. Therefore, we should talk about . . .

Boots

Most important of all your gear is footwear. The selection of boots depends on your needs. Let's start with the day hiker who is going on easy trails with a small pack or no pack at all. He can probably get by with tennis shoes or work boots. But beware the desert floor in the summer! When the ground temperature rises from 150 to 200 degrees Fahrenheit, the heat will come up through the tennies and make hot spots mighty quick on the bottoms of bathtub-smooth pinkies. A pair of lightweight hiking boots is better because these give feet more protection against the hot desert floor. And who knows—you may decide some fine day to leave the trail and do some exploring. That's the first sign of a future backpacker.

Good Vibram-type rubber soles and good arch and ankle support are both needed for off-trail wandering. Tennies just don't give you that. Some old, grizzled desert rats I know swear by tennis shoes. But here again, if the tennis shoe fits, wear it. You are the ultimate decision maker. I mean, I've seen people start down Bright Angel Trail, heading for the bottom of the Grand Canyon, in clogs, sandals, high-risers, deckers, and bare feet. They keep the mules busy and put coins in the cowboys' pockets when they have to be hauled out.

There are many good manufacturers of quality, lightweight boots. I would stay away from the $29.95 specials. Expect to pay from $50 to $100 for a good pair. You might find some satisfactory light boots at a surplus or discount store for $30 or so. Consider U.S. army surplus Vietnam boots. They would carry you into moderate backpacking.

Okay. You decide you want to venture farther into the unknown and sleep overnight on the desert. You are now a backpacker and must carry additional weight that will all settle onto the bottoms of your feet. Try it with the light-weight boots. If they serve the purpose, good. If you think you need more support, and are going to become a long-term backpacker, you may wish to consider a mediumweight boot with a thicker sole. Most boot manufacturers' catalogs give you a good breakdown on the different boot models and their purposes. Unless you will be spending six months crossing

MERRELL "Mariah" GTX hiking boot. Courtesy Karhu USA.

the Gobi Desert, the most boot you will need for dry-land wanderings will be a mediumweight. But try a heavyweight on anyway just to know how one feels.

In general, Italian boots are made to fit more comfortably when new than German, Swiss, or Austrian boots. If numbers mean anything, the consistently most popular desert hiking boot sold in the High Adventure stores from 1969 to 1975 was the Italian-made Fabiano 360, followed by the Vasque Cascade. There are many comparable boots and you should sample as many as possible before buying.

Let's talk about fit. Rare is the perfect fit. Generally, the softer, more padded boot fits better and feels more comfortable at first. Every pair of feet is different. I have fitted hundreds of pairs of boots, including a ladies' size 15 wide and a men's size 6 medium. If we all walked barefoot, we could identify each other by our foot differences as well as our face differences.

Have your foot measured on a Brannock device in the store. Pay no attention to your street or golf shoe size. Determine the foot width at its widest part and then note the width of your heel. If the heel of your foot is narrow and the ball wide, you are in trouble. You may have to compromise by getting a boot that fits the ball width, then wear two pairs of heavy socks to make the heel snug. One overlooked key to proper boot fit is the lacing technique. With a narrow heel and wide foot, for example, you can tie the lace off at the point where the boot starts up the front of your foot. Then you can pull the top part in very snugly without affecting the wider part of your boot. Each brand of boot, and each style within each brand, fits a bit differently. Even the same sizes in the same models can feel different on your feet.

When trying on a size, put on at least one pair of heavy wool socks first. Slide your foot forward in the boot until the toes fit up against the inside. Bend your knees forward and try

Lightweight hiking boots with combination leather and waterproof fabrics. Photo by Aimee Madsen, courtesy of Asolo and Vasque.

to stick two fingers all the way down between your heel and the heel of the boot. It should fit snugly. Now lace the boot up in the manner described. Put on both boots. Try to push your toes into the front by holding the boot against a wall and sliding your foot forward. Your toes should not touch. If they do, try lacing your boots a bit tighter and try the wall trick again. Walk around the store to get the general feel of the boot. Does the heel feel snug? Is there ample room for your toes to spread and flex? Walk up some stairs and feel whether your heel slides up and down inside the boot. Next, try on the same boot a half size narrower and then a half size wider, going through the same test routine.

Buy the boots of your choice on the condition that you can wear them around the house for a week, checking for fit. Don't take them out in the dirt until you are sure you will keep them. New boots work loose, so you must relace them often to get a snug fit. You may feel some hot spots developing on your heel, on the ball of your foot, or on your toes. Put some plain one-inch adhesive tape or some Moleskin over these spots to keep the boot from rubbing the skin. Let's face it, you are wearing something different from your usual street shoes or sandals. There will be some breaking-in time for all new boots.

If, after wearing them around the house, you are satisfied the boots will work out, start walking up and down some hills or your local training mountain. If by accident you step through some water or get rained on, wear the boots until they dry. You will be amazed how fast they break in or conform to your feet when wet. After all, it's a combination of perspiration plus friction that breaks them in anyway. As a matter of fact, if you are in a hurry or have trouble getting the boots to break in, soak them in warm water for fifteen minutes and wear them dry. Then put the recommended leather preservative on them.

Most boot manufacturers recommend a particular leather conditioner for their boots. Use it. You are protecting an investment. Find out who repairs and resoles hiking boots. Go and talk to him, and ask his advice concerning boot maintenance.

When you start getting used to the boots, put a pack on with 20 pounds weight and do some more hill climbing. You will perhaps find your foot sliding into the toe of your boot on the downhill. Work with the laces again to snug in the heel.

After a trip, clean your boots with warm water and a nylon brush. Get the dirt out of seams and welt areas. Let wet boots dry in the house. Heat is the worst enemy of leather boots, so don't ever dry boots by a fire or in the sun. Don't put boots in the trunk of your car when driving in desert country. I have seen boots curl up like caterpillars because the hikers wore them through wet country in northern Arizona then put them in the trunk to drive back to Phoenix. In the Lower Sonoran Desert, where the air temperature is 120 degrees Fahrenheit, the trunk turned into an oven and baked the boots.

On long hikes carry extra shoelaces and a least two rolls of one-inch-wide adhesive tape for repairs. The tape will hold almost anything together in an emergency. I was hiking with a friend in the Superstitions when her boots began to fall apart. The soles and midsoles separated from the uppers. We taped the soles to the uppers and kept the boots together long enough to get back to town—and get a refund.

When you stop for breaks during a desert hike, take off your boots and shake out the dirt and dust from your socks. Soak your feet if you are by a stream, and give them a rubdown. Better yet, do an exchange foot rub with a friend. Let your feet dry thoroughly and use foot powder. I cannot overemphasize the need for proper foot care both before and during a hike. If you plan on nothing more than a day hike, you still need to get your feet in shape. Desert hiking can fry your feet due to the hot, hard, unforgiving terrain. Keep your toenails trim and clean. And don't go barefoot around camp. Carry a light pair of tennies, moccasins, or muk-luks for camp wear. This gives your feet a break and keeps your boots away from the campfire.

Socks

Heavy wool socks are my favorite hiking companions—second only to a good foot massager. They cushion, protect, absorb moisture, keep feet warm if needed, and otherwise treat feet right. With light hiking, I usually wear one pair; with heavy hiking, two pair. There are many combinations of inner liners: thin wool, synthetics, cotton, and silk. Try them all if you have the money, but I think you will find that wool is best in the long run. Wigwam Mills puts out a small pamphlet on socks and wool.

Carry two or three pairs of socks, alternating once a day for best foot comfort. Hang the used pair on your pack to dry while hiking. If plenty of water is available, rinse them out at

Good hiking socks by Wigwam: the Mohave is 100% wool; the El-Pine is 85% wool, 13% nylon and 2% Spandex; the Trek is 50% polypropylene, 40% wool and 10% nylon. Photo by Aimee Madsen, courtesy Wigwam Mills.

night. Forget about soap until you get home. Do not rinse them directly in a stream or pool; rinse them on the bank. Remember, water is precious in the desert, and there should be no reason to contaminate any water source.

Years ago, Jerry Robertson and I were on our second attempt of Mt. Sinyala in the Grand Canyon. We were carrying fifty-pound packs (damn climbing gear). We tried everything to cut down weight. I decided to wear my climbing shoes for the entire trip. We usually wore hiking boots to our canyon destinations and carried our close-fitting rock shoes for sandstone-tower scaling. Anyway, I had been hiking and running before the trip to get my feet in shape, and I thought they were tough. It's a good thing I had carried my trusty, all-purpose roll of adhesive tape. By the time we got to the sandstone temple, my feet looked like those of an Egyptian mummy. The tape kept them from completely disintegrating. I hobbled all the way back to Supai—two days of cross-country, heavy-pack misery. I sent my pack up to the rim from Supai on the back of a mule. They seldom get blisters.

Sleeping Bag

I remember when you could buy a surplus army sleeping bag for ten dollars. It weighed about a pound per dollar, was filled with God-knows-what kind of feathers, always stank, and was always olive drab in color. But that was the best backpacking bag available then, unless you were in the upper income bracket that could afford an Eddie Bauer bag.

Now there is a wide selection of designs, comfort ranges, weights, colors, and prices. A sleeping bag is a major purchase, and you should be well informed. There is not enough room in this book to go into all the technical details of sleeping bags, so we'll just stick to the basics.

The most important question to think about when you are shopping for a sleeping bag is: What are your short-range and long-range needs? If you are going out no more than a couple times, it makes no economic sense to buy a good bag unless you expect to pass it on to someone else. Rent one; or if you have a very good friend, borrow one. All right, you've been out a couple times and you dig it. Time to shop for a good one. The question now is: What range of temperature will you be getting into? Will you stay in the low deserts during the fall, winter, and spring? Will you venture into the mountains, or become a winter camper, extending your range into the subzero class? Think about this before you go shopping. Keep in mind also that there are now bag combinations on the market whereby you can purchase a light bag that will fit inside a heavier bag at a later date, giving you three possible ranges.

Good sleeping bags are filled with goose down, duck down, or a combination of the two. Good sleeping bags are also filled with different synthetics, their design and performance every bit as good as down, with the exception of weight and bulk. There has been so much controversy and marketing hoopla over the various qualities of goose versus duck down over the years, that one hardly knows whether to quack or honk. There is raw goose down, raw duck down, raw goose-duck combinations, garment grade, bag grade, superior grade, AA grade, Northern European, Prime Canadian, 100 percent down, 80 percent, 50 percent, no percent (the manufacturers thought sure that chicken feathers constituted down), cold weather goose down, colder weather duck down, clean down, dirty down, white down, brown down, and last but not least, black down. The real sources of down have always been somewhat of a mystery to consumers and dealers alike. It seems that China has been supplying quite a bit for years, passing it through Europe, Taiwan, or Canada. Most of the bag manufacturers get it from the same suppliers anyway. If you stick with better-known brands, you can hardly go wrong as long as you do some homework and study the catalogs. Most good manufacturers guarantee their bags. If you buy a bag that is rated to twenty degrees Fahrenheit and you happen to go up to Colorado and sleep out in zero-degree weather, don't blame the store salesman if you get cold. Planning for the coldest possibility is part of your climate control plan.

Synthetic bags are going through progressive evolutions now due to the higher costs of obtaining and processing

The Cat's Meow, three-season bag; three pounds, six ounces of PolarGuard. Photo by Aimee Madsen, courtesy The North Face.

down. Polarguard, Fiberfill, Quallofil and Hollofil II, seem to be the front-runners in the quality bag market. In general, until a major breakthrough takes place, a good synthetic-fill bag is about 30 percent heavier, 30 percent bulkier, and 30 to 50 percent cheaper than a good down bag. Synthetics will maintain up to 70 percent efficiency when wet, whereas down will lose most of its loft under the same conditions. This is an overstated problem, however, unless you are doing a lot of ice and snow climbing or a lot of backpacking in the rainy West Coast climate. For the desert, and 90 percent of the rest of the hiking you will do, either type will fill the bill.

Foam-filled bags have been used with some success in

wetter, colder climates. They get a bit clammy inside but provide you with a built-in mattress. Due to their spongy protection, they make excellent mountain rescue bags for lowering, hauling, and keeping a victim warm. Foam bags have not really been perfected yet, but I believe they have a great future.

Wool blankets? You bet! I can remember many nights of my youth when a couple of wool army blankets wrapped in canvas made for a pleasant—well, tolerable—night's sleep. They are used regularly by desert rats on river running and rafting trips down the Colorado, San Juan, Green, and other western rivers.

Size is another factor. It is a good idea to buy a bag longer than you are. You can snuggle down into it on extra-cold or windy nights. You can stuff the foot end with clothing, boots, water bottles, anything that you want to protect from the elements. Make sure you feel comfortable with the shoulder width. Mummy bags are tapered, form-fit bags that cut down weight and cost. A rectangular bag is roomier, heavier, and costlier. Make sure the bag has a two-way zipper for warm weather ventilation. Measure the loft-to-weight ratios for the best indication of fill content.

After you have read all the catalogs and books that you can stand, go back through the stores and start trying some on for size. By now the salespeople will either hide when they see you coming or rise to the challenge to serve you and gain your confidence. Either way, they will be less likely to try to snow you since you will be so well informed. Make sure the bag comes with a heavy-duty nylon stuff sack. Don't settle for a cheap one.

When you are out in the field, air your bag in the morning before stuffing it. Do not smoke in it, or lay it near a campfire or stove. If you are expecting rain, take along a large garbage bag as a double protection to use when stuffing the bag into the stuff sack.

As you have undoubtedly guessed by now, desert hiking involves a great deal of sidestepping around the ouches and ooches from needle-sharp plant appendages. Mesquite trees,

The Blue Kazoo, a lightweight down bag suitable for most mild-weather desert overnight hiking; weighs two pounds. Photo by Aimee Madsen, courtesy The North Face.

catclaws, and cholla cactus have a penchant for hanging onto parkas, sleeping bags, and bare legs. If you carry your bag tied onto the bottom of your pack frame, use two heavy-duty nylon stuff sacks. And remember, when you put your bag out on the ground, always put a ground cloth down first.

I guess it is obvious by now that I love to tell stories. Here's one that should convice you to never go on an overnight hike without a sleeping bag.

A few years ago, Steve Williams, Dan Bingham, and I were climbing Zoroaster Temple, a sandstone juggernaut in the Grand Canyon. We were not in the best physical shape, so we decided to leave all our gear except bivouac and climbing hardware on the Tonto Plateau. We had 4,000 more vertical feet to go to reach the summit. It was Easter, and there was snow on the higher ledges of the inner canyon. Snow meant water. It also meant cold. But we decided to sacrifice warmth for weight and left our sleeping bags on the plateau also. We bivouaced two nights, curled around small fires. We used thin, flat pieces of sandstone to direct the heat toward our bodies. The first night when I tried to move the pieces of sandstone, I found they were hot on both sides. That gave us an idea. We laid a couple of heated pieces down flat and laid our bodies on them. Glory be! A warm bed. We found we could lay a third one on top of our bellies and heat our topsides as well. They would retain their warmth for about an hour, and in the meantime others would be heating. We stayed awake in shifts, keeping the fire going. We had invented the backpacker's electric blanket! We decided, however, that the next time we would take sleeping bags.

Between the Bag and the Ground

The desert is not necessarily soft, comfy sand. It is usually hard clay, crushed granite, mineral soil, or other durable concoction. No pine-needle beds or soft forest floor here. I mean, there is nothing soft in the desert except a velvet ant's behind, and I wouldn't advise you to pet one.

Some climbing friends sleep on coiled ropes and packs. Other hardy men I know sleep on the bare ground after they've softened it with a piton hammer and a boot heel. Whatever the method, you will probably be restless the first night.

There are many air mattresses and foam pads on the market, so you have quite a selection. Air-filled mattresses run the gamut from cheap plastic, which I do not recommend, to high quality, military standard, rubber-coated canvas. Collapsibility is both the advantage and disadvantage of an air mattress. The advantage is that it is compact to carry; the disadvantage is obvious if you spring a leak in the middle of a cold night. But an air mattress also floats and can take you across a river or small body of water in a pinch. Foam pads come in many lengths, thicknesses, and price ranges. Ensolite types of closed-cell foam are waterproof and lightweight but provide a minimum of comfort. Thicker, open-celled foam is not waterproof, and therefore must be protected with a waterproof nylon cover. But they are usually more comfortable than the closed-cell foam. Self-inflating mattresses add a new dimension to ground softeners. So the choice is a matter of preference between

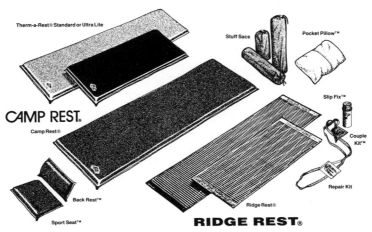

Camp Rest and Therm-a-Rest mattresses. Courtesy of Camp Rest.

comfort, convenience, weight, and price. Just remember, one good night's sleep may be worth a few extra dollars. Take as big a pad as you enjoy sleeping on. Later, when your rear end, shoulders, and hips get tough, you can get by with a shorter, thinner mattress. I slept on a one-eighth-inch-thick pad for 21 days in Wyoming. That is only a little thicker than a corn tortilla. It took a week to get used to.

A good friend and river rat, Big Daddy Ross Clements—I call him Big Daddy because he reminds me of a wrestler—bought a top-quality air mattress from our store when I was in the business. Seems he would run a river, then bring the mattress back with the seams torn apart. We would give him a new one and send the defective one back to the factory for credit. This happened three times in a row and I couldn't figure out why these highly respected mattresses were defective. Well sir, I went on a river trip with Ross and found out. Big Daddy was 220 pounds if he was an ounce, and he bellowed like a bear when he issued commands. Nobody argued with him—except his air mattress. After all the chores were taken care of, Ross liked to flop down and comtemplate the waning sunlight and beginning starlight. And when Ross flopped, he would literally fall on his mattress with a 220-pound, gravity-fed "whomp" that could pin Strangler Lewis. A week of falling Ross would blow the seams out of a welded mattress.

Tents and Tarps

My favorite shelter in the desert is God's canopy of starlight, which I can lie under and watch for shooting stars, satellites, and UFOs. The majority of desert rats I know do not carry tents in the desert lowlands. There simply is not enough bad weather to warrant the weight except during a prolonged winter storm. A tube tent or tarp will usually suffice for those brief wettings during the summer.

What about creepies and crawlies and snakes? I have never heard of anyone being attacked by a tarantula, scorpion, or jackrabbit. If you lay your tarp over their home, then sure, they are liable to get a bit hostile. That's why it's best not to wait until night to make camp. Every survival book I have ever read cautions you to check your boots in the morning to see whether a leather-loving scorpion has bivouacked in the toe for the night. But the only time I heard of anyone finding a scorpion in his shoe was when my mother found one in her

EUREKA Tent-Aurora. Courtesy of Johnson Camping.

bedroom slipper. It got her, too. I have to admit, though, I still shake my boots out. The idea that a snake wants to sleep with you is also pretty ridiculous. I'm sure he would prefer his own kind. The only desert critters I know who like to crawl on *Homo sapiens* are the eternal ants and mosquitoes and those occasional no-see-'ems. Mosquitoes are few in the desert unless you are near pools or streams.

There is one little family of creatures that can enter your food supply uninvited. They are rock rats, little, furry, sharp-toothed rodents that will sometimes eat right out of your hand. They will also eat right through your nylon and plastic baggies to get at the vanilla pudding, brown sugar, and other sweets.

If you prefer the privacy of a tent, consider the mosquito-net-walled tents with fly. They are airy and light; they keep condensation to a minimum and provide a great view of the constellations with the fly off.

Eureka Crescent one- or two-man tent. Courtesy Eureka Tent Co.

A strong, waterproof, nylon tarp is my favorite desert shelter. Versatile, light, and less expensive than a tent, this all-purpose item can be modified to desires of the most creative shelter maker. With grommet-reinforced holes, a tarp can be tied to anything. A hiking staff or stick can prop up the middle like a circus tent. Rain shelter, sun shade, wind barrier—its utility is limited only by your imagination. Tarps come in various sizes from many manufacturers. Or you can make one easily from a kit, or buy the components to design one yourself.

Packboard ponchos, those extra-long ponchos that fit over packs, usually have grommets and snaps for conversion to tarp use. The hood hole can be tied off. A couple of ponchos snapped together can make a great shelter for two, reminiscent of the old army buddy-system tent.

Caves

Caves are okay if you don't mind the possibility of sharing. Other creatures like caves, too, and you just might be stepping into someone's home. If you see nests or lots of scat—then *you* scat and make your bed elsewhere. Small niches and washed-out places under sandstone ledges make great little caves with projecting roofs for weary hikers to snuggle under.

As mentioned before, dry washes, arroyos, and streambeds should be avoided when looking for camping spots. I have seen a normally docile canyon creek turn into a rampaging monster after a local cloudburst. I once stood ankle deep in one of these creeks, looking 20 feet up the slope to the high level it had reached the week before. Tree trunks a foot in diameter were bent at ninety-degree angles or snapped in two. Bushes and shrubs were stripped clean of leaves. Pieces of a Volkswagen were twisted around a tree trunk. An inch-thick steel trailer beam was circled around another tree. Enough said.

Odds and Ends

You cannot plan for every possible contingency on a desert hike or you will need a burro to carry the weight. You will have to set your own priorities about what is worth carrying and what is not. Here are some items that I think are worth the space they take in a pack.

Carry two flashlights with spare batteries and extra bulbs. It's wise to be prepared for really dark, cloudy nights or emergency situations when a good light is indispensable. Be sure to check the bulbs, batteries, and switches of your flashlights before each trip; these things have a nasty habit of just giving up.

A knife is a very personal thing. I have a friend who carries one as big as a machete and another friend who takes one as small as your little finger. Pocket knives are okay as long as they are big enough to slice bread and cheese, cut tough nylon cord and leather, and dice up a carrot. Belt knives come in a hundred shapes and sizes. A well-designed knife is a thing of beauty. One of these days I will spend $100 and get one handmade. If you leave home with a newly sharpened, honed blade, you will seldom need to sharpen it again on a short backpack trip. For a week or more in the wilds, you might want to carry a sharpening stone. I carry a three-inch bladed folding knife on my belt and a small, all-purpose pocket knife that has a nail cleaner and clipper, tweezers, and scissors.

How about pack repair in the field? A supply of plain adhesive tape is a must. I have used it to repair an aluminum frame that had cracked at nearly every joint after it was dropped with a heavy load attached. The tape held the frame together, with 50 pounds of pack weight, for a week. Carry an extra set of pins and rings if the system uses them. If a grommet pulls out, you can always punch a hole in the nylon bag edge and tie the pack onto the frame with a piece of parachute cord. Other valuable repair kit items are a razor blade, ripstop repair tape, and glue. I always carry at least fifty feet of

> Not to have known either the mountain or the desert is not to have known one's self. Not to have known oneself is to have known no one.
>
> —Joseph Wood Krutch

*Backpacker II pocketknife with tweezers.
Courtesy of Precise International.*

Buck finger-grooved knives. Courtesy Buck Knives.

nylon parachute cord for various tie-together situations. It can replace broken shoelaces, tie up tarps, or repair a pack frame.

A small trowel is good to have for latrine and cookout duty. A few feet of surgical tubing is great for syphoning water from potholes and shallow streams. A comb and tweezers come in handy for removing cholla cactus needles.

For backpacking nightlife and for reading and writing, a well-protected candle is nice to have. Related to this are a good book to read, pens and a small notebook in which to keep records of the trip, and a disposable butane lighter—along with your waterproof matches.

I like to bring along a small pair of binoculars so that I can zero in on wildlife, landforms, water holes, and other landmarks. And to most people, camera gear is a must. Special care must be taken to protect this expensive stuff from the elements. Keep this gear in a plastic bag or a waterproof pouch to protect it from rain and dust. I have had to have my 35mm lens cleaned three times due to fine desert dust that worked its way into the shutter, rings, and bearings. Be sure to carry a brush, lens cleaner, and tissue, too.

A Pack to Put It In

There are now so many backpack designs that it makes one stand in awe of anyone who could have carried an army A-frame, a Trapper Nelson, or a tumpline. It is quite possible that you could never see all of the new models because by the time you went through them, ten new ones would be on the market. Despite the continuing stream of new backpack designs, I think the state of the art of frame and bag design has now reached a point of diminishing returns. Still, a few of the new trends are worth discussing here.

Among the latest improvements in pack design have been the larger, internal frame and bag combinations in which there are no exposed aluminum pieces or edges separate from the pack itself. The majority of the units on the market have some sort of flexible aluminum, plastic, or nylon braces that are sewn vertically inside the pack with horizontal stabilizers. The suspension systems have been improving steadily and in some cases have surpassed the external frame and bag combi-nations. In general, the flexibility of the internal braces or frame allows you to bend the vertical pieces to form-fit to your back and upper shoulders. This puts pack weight closer to your center of gravity, but the tradeoff is a hotter back in desert hiking. Check the carrying volumes of each pack you try on. Give the internal frame packs the same walk-around test as the external combinations.

An important development has been the padded hip belt designed to transfer some of the weight from the shoulders and back to the hipbones. It always ended up there anyway but now there is less stress on all those troublemaking vertebrae in between. The forward-lift suspension system, or wraparound frame, was hailed by the engineers as a break-through. But alas, engineers look upon human bodies as machines that all work the same way. Have you ever seen two people who walk exactly the same way? We all carry our bodies slightly differently when we walk. Therefore, no pack and frame combination is going to fit any two people the same way. Some folks can wear a forward-lift suspension pack comfortably, some can't. Some folks like a wide hip belt, some a narrow one. Some folks wear neither, carrying the brunt of the load on their shoulders. Are they stupid, uninformed, traditional? None of the above. Some have tried all the new innovations and simply feel more comfortable in the old-style frame.

So let the charts, diagrams, and arrows be damned. Don't let anyone tell you what feels comfortable to you. Try on differ-ent systems carrying twenty pounds or more, and walk around in the store. Go up and down stairs, climb on the roof. You could even try squeezing into the bathroom to get a feel for what it's like to get through high, close boulders. Lean forward, sideways, and backward. Take it off and put it on two or three times.

Now before you get stuck between the sink and the toilet bowl, let's talk about simplicity of design and proper fitting techniques. The key to fit is the suspension system: shoulder straps, back bands, and hip belt. These determine how the weight of the pack will ride on your body. The tighter the weight hugs your body, the closer it is to your own center of gravity, and the easier it is to move in all directions.

When you are trying on a pack read the manufacturer's instructions to make sure you have everything where it should be. A suspension system designed to go over your shoulders and extend down over your back for an inch or two is more efficient than one that comes straight out from the frame and slopes over the front of your shoulders. A padded hip belt should rest with about one inch extending above your hipbone and the other two or three inches on the hipbone itself. The back band should fit snugly and securely. I prefer mesh back bands because they ventilate heat better than solid ones, and desert hiking calls for much ventilation. With 20 or 30 pounds in the pack, adjust the shoulder straps so they extend over your shoulders. Cinch up the hip belt and walk around. The weight should be evenly distributed between shoulders and hips. The hip belt should be riding on the outward-sloping part of the rump. If the shoulder straps are in place and the hip belt rides up over the waist, the suspension system is too short for you. If the hip belt buckle rides so low as to feel like a steel jockstrap or chastity belt, the system is too long.

Many new frame and bag combinations now have a range of suspension adjustments from small to extra large. This is a sensible innovation since you should have your choice of bag size no matter what size you are. Get the biggest bag available. You can always carry less in a big bag but must resort to tie-ons in order to carry more in a small bag.

Pack bags come in all sizes and shapes, but let's stick to basics. The more complex the bag, the more problems it can give you. Unless you are the type of person who always has a place for everything and keeps everything in its place, I do not recommend starting with a multipocket bag. Consider an old-style, straight-through bag with a couple of side pockets and perhaps a map pocket. An extendable top will give you extra room for larger loads. A vertical frame extension serves the same purpose. Much beyond this is luxury.

CAMP TRAILS "Orion" backpack. Courtesy of Johnson Camping.

sideways terrain, and for boulder hopping, keep the weight closer to the middle. For steep climbing, put the heavier stuff in the bottom. It is much simpler to do this by rearranging stuff sacks than by zipping and unzipping compartments, trying to fit large items in dividers, or dumping the entire contents on the ground and putting it back in piece by piece.

Organize your gear in separate stuff sacks, using different colors for toilet articles, clothing, cooking gear, and such. Then put the stuff sacks in the pack bag the way you find most convenient. For most straight and level walking, put the heavier weight on top. For cross-country, up-and-down, and

CAMP TRAILS "Cornice" backpack. Courtesy of Johnson Camping.

Ah, but here I am telling you what to do, against my basic philosophy of letting you learn for yourself. Let's just say that I am suggesting. I have watched from the rim of the Grand Canyon as people headed down into her depths carrying kids and pussycats on their shoulders, dogs in their arms, and guitars and banjos on their packs. I've seen people carrying nothing but a quart of milk in a paper sack; and I've seen people hauling wheeled carts behind them. I have even seen a couple of people barefoot. Who am I to say what's right for you? I would much rather see a group of people with all different kinds and colors of packs and paraphernalia—as long as they were comfortable, having fun, and respecting the environment—than I would a boring string of all-the-sames who are hiking by somebody else's school solution. I have seen too many grim faces, eyes staring at the ground, legs hell-bent on doing too many miles for the day. To each his or her own. You will work out your own refinements from other readings, from campfire debates, and from keeping track of what you forgot or took too much of on the last trip.

For a simple day hike, you can get by with any one of a hundred different models of small, light, one- or two-compartment packs. They are easy to make in kit form. These day hike bags range in size from the Camp Trails *Mee Too* for the toddler to the larger size rucksacks used for climbing, ski touring, and other less-than-overnight camping trips.

5

Desert Kitchen Plan

. . . Green chili jelly is delicious.

What to eat in the wilderness? There are as many approaches to food as there are individual tastes. Some people like to eat like gourmets, some like Spartans. Some folks have nothing but freeze-dried foods to limit weight, and others carry aluminum dutch ovens just to exhibit their biscuit-baking prowess.

There are few "shoulds" when it comes to food, and it's a fine idea to experiment. I have a friend who wraps a whole chicken in aluminum foil in the morning, puts it on top of his pack and hikes all day in the summertime with the Arizona sun beating down on him and his chicken. He swears to me that the chicken is baked by the time he makes camp. I haven't hiked with him so I can't attest to the story's validity. Maybe he stops by Colonel Sander's first and just keeps the chicken warm during the hike. In order to give you a good idea of the wide latitude in food planning preferences—I'll start this chapter with a few quotes and episodes about wilderness menus.

A Matter of Taste
"There are no doubt a few places in which certain select souls could live off the land and still find time to do one or two

other things as well, but my advice is to leave the happy dreams to those who have never tried it . . .

"In choosing what foods to take, consider:

1. Nutritional values, especially stick-to-gutability
2. Weight
3. Ease of preparation
4. Palatability
5. Packaging (with special thought for litter)
6. Cost

"On every account, except cost, the only answer is dehydrated food—either freeze-dried or vacuum dried. Less than two and a quarter pounds of it can satisfy your nutritional needs for a highly energetic day."

Colin Fletcher

"I try to live off the land as much as possible when I backpack. I've tried to eat almost everything on the desert, experimenting slowly with each plant and berry. On my two-week cross-country desert survival trip, I ate Saguaro fruit, chia seeds, mesquite beans and pods, peas from the ironwood tree, hackberries, tomatillos, yellow monkey flowers, water-cress, wild spearmint, wild dandelion, prickly pear fruit, crawfish from the Verde river, creosote, ephedra and broom tea, sprouted palo verde peas, and a mixture of mashed jojoba nuts that I made into patties and carried in my pack. I lost 15 pounds, but I made it."

A quote from Peter Busnack,
carpenter and survival instructor in
Phoenix, Arizona

"Check the catalog of any store that carries a complete line of dehydrated and freeze-dried dishes. They read like the fantasy of a starving man: Tuna à la Neptune, Chili Con Carne Ranchero, Beef Almondine [sic], Turkey Tetrazini [sic], Chicken Chop Suey—they've got to be kidding. Then there are packaged menus for breakfast, lunch, dinner, snacks, and desserts that go the same way. The whole American food trip freeze-dried. It seems something better could be thought up, something more in keeping with the spirit of wilderness. How long can we go on using a gift of such beauty as fire to cook up freeze-dried Turkey Supreme? Even white flour bisquits [*sic*], bacon grease, and coffee have more the feeling of proper outdoor grub."

> Albert Saijo in his book,
> *The Backpacker*

Saijo emphasizes lightweight, concentrated foods such as seeds, nuts, grain, dried fruits, health-food store fare, Japanese and other foreign foods, and gourmet cheeses.

Jerry Robertson and I spent four days climbing Mt. Sinyala—an isolated desert peak near Havasu Canyon. It was June and it was hot, and we were carrying all our water. To cut down on weight, we decided to carry just enough food to survive. Jerry put together a concoction of wheat germ, protein powder, powdered milk, raisins, nuts—and God knows what else—in an oatmeal carton, which we labeled "Swill." Mixed with water, that was just about our entire feed for the four days. Not much on taste, but we kept our energy and made the climb.

The National Outdoor Leadership School program, recommends dry, nonperishable, easily transportable foods that do not include canned goods, foil-wrapped foods, prepackaged meals, fresh meat, or produce. They select a wide variety of foods with the proper caloric content and food balance, figuring about two pounds per person per day, then give you about a week's supply. *You* decide how much of what and when to eat each day. No daily menu is made up, giving imagination and experimentation full reign. The NOLS basic fare includes: dried milk, cheese, margarine, Bisquick mix, white and wheat flour, cornmeal, pasta, rice, barley, cereals, wheat germ, popcorn, dried vegetables and meat substitutes,

fruits and nuts, sugar, honey, puddings, cake mixes, coffee, tea, cocoa, fruit crystals, beef, chicken, and tomato bases, all kinds of spices, and whatever natural foods they run across in the wilderness. They emphasize this approach for large groups and extended trips. Weekenders usually find it easier to use prepackaged foods because they are normally pressed for time on a two-day trip.

In the summer of 1975, I went on an NOLS outdoor educator's course and spent twenty days on a great cross-country trip near the Tetons of Wyoming. My tent partner and I came up with some interesting combinations for meals—some good, some bad, and some buried. We were going to bake a pizza on coals for the first dinner. We rolled out the dough with our fishing-pole case, popped it in the pan, and waited. It soon rose up, lifted the lid off the pan, and stabilized at three inches. We covered it with tomato sauce, reconstituted mushrooms, cheese, and spices, and invented the "pizza pound cake." Try asking for one of those at your local pizza parlor.

I personally like a mixture of dried and fresh foods. My most memorable delicacies have been: a fresh orange on the summit of the Angel's Gate sandstone temple in the Grand Canyon; fresh cantaloupe for breakfast on top of Weaver's Needle; a juicy celery stick in the middle of a hot day in Saguaro National Monument. We have taken fresh sliced ham and beef, cheeses, carrots, celery, peppers, even tomatoes, on a three-day hike in the desert in the spring. We put most fresh items in the freezer the night before our trip, then bury them in the middle of our packs inside plastic containers the next day. We make dinner soup of the melted water.

Yet another food approach is that of the no-cook option. You can make various, and very delicious, pemmican conglomerations ahead of time and combine these with fruits, vegetables, seeds, nuts, grain, cheeses, and whatever else that strikes your fancy to free you from any cooking chores—and also free you from the weight of stoves, fuel, and utensils.

Eating desert plants can supplement and add a note of originality to any desert menu. I have stained my whole face purple from the juice of the prickly pear fruit. (I have listed a couple good books on edible desert plants in the Appendix.) But forget about wild animals. Too much energy will be expended in catching wild game, and, what's more important, wildlife can be diseased, can bite, sting, and stab. Leave your guns at home.

You must be getting hungry by now. Go bake yourself a loaf of bread, and while the oven is doing its job, whip up some *green chili jelly* to spread on it.

RECIPE: 4 long green chilis   drain
           1 bell pepper   and
           1 jalapeno pepper   c/c seed

           1¼ cups vinegar

Liquefy ingredients in blender.
Put results in pan with 5 cups sugar. Bring to boil
and skim. Add 1 bottle Certo, stir, and boil 2
minutes.
Add a few drops of green coloring.
Serve with cream cheese.

So, you've decided that the first night out you will have a
seven-course Italian dinner. Well, for sure you will need . . .

Some Basics

There are four food groups: dairy products (include cheese,
milk, and yogurt); grains (such as wheat, rice, rye, and barley);
fruits and vegetables; and proteins (such as meat, eggs, and
nuts). On a long trip, you should include some of each food
group in your meal planning for variety and nutrition. (I have
listed some good backpack cookery books in the Appendix.)

Utensils

I have never seen any two backpackers carrying the same
utensils. Pots, pans, bottles, containers, cups, and plates come
in an endless variety of sizes, shapes, and utility. I have gone
for days with nothing more than a spoon and cup. I have also
been on a three-week trip where we carried frying pans,
spatulas, mixing spoons—even a small tea pot. Just like the
food, it depends on the trip and what you like to eat. I know
some folks who eat nothing on their weekend trips. They are
determined to lose weight, and, if they take no food, they are
on a forced diet. Then again, I have hauled a birthday cake,
champagne, cantaloupe, steaks, and fresh vegetables up to the
top of Weaver's Needle in the Superstition Mountains in order
to celebrate a birthday. Just remember, the more fancy you get, the
more weight you have to carry on your back.

It's fun to scour the catalogs for utensil ideas, but there are
just as many possibilities in your local supermarket and
variety store. Save all the plastic containers you get with foods
you buy—margarine containers, pill bottles, plastic milk

Five-piece aluminum mess kit. Courtesy of Palco Products.

bottles. They will come in handy for backpacking condiments such as tea, coffee, powdered milk, cocoa, and margarine. If you know a nurse, ask her to get you some throw-away saline solution bottles used in hospitals. These are one- and two-liter polyethylene rectangular beauties that are even marked off in milliliters.

I have used almost every plastic bottle that has come out on the market and am now testing these as to their ability to withstand freezing. I fill the bottle about four-fifths full, leave the cap off, and put it in the freezer overnight. I take it out for the next day's hike, top it off with fresh water, and stick it in the pack. It will gradually melt but will stay cold most of the day.

Some people have bad luck with plastic bottles due to leakage, and consequently condemn them all. Many times they have overtightened the lid and stripped the threads, causing the leaks. Other times they have put a plastic bottle close to a fire or stove, which results in a small melt hole. And, at times, there will be a bad run of bottles from the manufacturer. Here are my suggestions. Take the bottle into the bathroom at the store, fill it up with water, then hold it over your head and drop it. If it holds up, buy it. Fill it again at home, set it upside down for a couple days, and look for leaks. If it does leak, take it back.

Ross Clements tells a good story. He picked me up one late night after a party I had attended and was hauling me up to the San Juan River for my first river run. I had filled an old plastic army canteen full of good quality brandy to keep me warm while dodging icebergs during this cold December run. I put the canteen on the floor in the back and promptly fell asleep. The canteen had a very slow leak and the smell of that good quality brandy filled Ross's nostrils all the way to Mexican Hat, Utah. He did not know of the canteen and thought the brandy was oozing out of me as I slept. He couldn't believe anyone could drink so much and still be alive. When I discovered the canteen had lost all of its precious contents, I was fit to be tied and Ross was having a laughing fit. The moral of the story is to test and experiment *before* heading out.

The same holds true for cooking pots and pans. Try some out at home with your backpack stove. I am a fan of the one-pot dinner. I put a pot of tea water to boil, with twice as much water as I need for tea. I pour off the tea water into our cups and put soup ingredients into the remaining water. We enjoy our tea while the soup simmers. I add twice as much water to the soup as it boils, then pour it off, leaving the remaining soup as a base for the main dish. While we sip our soup, the macaroni, rice, beans, vegetables, meat, cheese, or whatever, is added and our main meal cooks. After the main meal is poured out, more water is boiled in the pot and it is either cleaned out and emptied or, in the case of a dry desert camp, poured out and consumed with a little Wyler's lemonade mix. The final pot of water rinses the pot and makes coffee.

Stoves

Since firewood is becoming more scarce in popular campgrounds, and fire danger is increasing due to the rapidly increasing numbers of back country travelers, backpack stoves are becoming necessary for cooking. They are also very convenient.

Some stoves burn white gas, some alcohol, some kerosene, some gasoline, some butane or propane; some burn solid fuel—and some don't burn at all. I have used just about all of them at one time or another, and the only generalization I can make is that they all have their own personalities—even among the same make and model; *especially* among the same make and model.

There are many tables and charts of stove comparisons such as fuel capacity, burning time, heat generated, weight, how long it takes to boil a quart of water, and so on. Take a look at the charts, then put them aside forever. Pick out the one that you *like* the most—the one that you have the best feeling about. Make friends with it. Take it home and provide a special place for it on the shelf. Give it a view, anything to keep it happy. For I firmly believe that stoves react to you as you treat them. They can be sweet, calm, efficient, and steady burning only to turn into irritable, mean, cantankerous, sputtering hunks of hot, heavy metal that you would just as soon kick over a cliff, especially when they turn on you in the middle of the main dish.

Learn to disassemble the stove in the dark. Keep it spotless at all times between trips. Take it apart after a trip and blow any hint of dust or dirt away, for it has been my experience that the main reason behind stove malfunctions is that they are not kept clean. Small particles of dust, dirt, and sand can clog orifices, pump, caps, generators, and fuel tank. Some

(Left) The Bleuet S-200. A compact, easy-to-pack camping stove. Courtesy of Wonder Corporation of America.

(Below) MSR Whisper-Lite white gas stove and Coleman Peak 1 multi-fuel stove. Photo by Aimee Madsen, courtesy of MSR and Coleman.

stoves come with a self-cleaning needle. If yours doesn't have one, buy a cleaning needle.

Colin Fletcher has tried almost all backpack stoves on the market and has made an exhaustive study on their performance. He still likes a Svea—he started with a Svea. It has become his friend. He has learned to master it (well, almost, because nobody ever learns to master a stove).

The National Outdoor Leadership School has put hundreds of youngsters out in the boonies for weeks on end with the Optimus 8R and 111B stoves. They have proven rugged and trustworthy. Well, almost. On my NOLS trip, my tent partner and I almost kicked ours over that cliff and cooked with fire. We hadn't taken time to become friends with it.

On our desert-rat expedition to Mt. McKinley, Alaska, we had chosen three Optimus 111B stoves, the favored stove for Mt. McKinley high-altitude climbing. They had proven themselves time and again with successful expeditions. Ours worked fine until we were holed up in an ice cave at 17,000 feet. Then they all stopped working at once. I lay in my sleeping bag for thirty-six hours—disassembling, cleaning, reassembling, pleading, cajoling, humoring, whispering, and cursing. It was too late. The stoves had decided they were not going to cook at this altitude and that was it. When we returned to 14,000 feet, they hummed along as if nothing had happened. We wrote Optimus, asked dozens of climbers, read all the reasons why there was no *real* reason why they should have failed—and just decided they must have been mad at us.

Fires

Fires are becoming a controversial subject among the 'new' backpackers. Weaned on a more conservation-oriented ethic than us older buzzards, they are more attuned to the hazards and visual pollution of campfires. Fires can be cozy, friendly, warming, and make good cook stoves. They can also cause desert scars that can be seen for miles, be the resting place for discarded cans, paper, foil, and cigarette butts, and can cause brush fires in densely vegetated areas. Burnable material is scarce in the desert. Dead cholla, saguaro, and other fallen plant stalks are home to many rodents, reptiles, and insects. But then again, fires have been basic to camping—and man himself—for millions of years. Campfires have always been accepted as part of the outdoor experience. And alas, the exploding population growth has imposed new restrictions on us for survival—and survival of the wild country. Hence, the controversy. Therefore, I will propose my own desert fire ethic.

A fire is justified if you leave no trace of it when you leave. Gather burnables from a wide area—not just in one spot so as to denude an area. Keep the fire small and burn only one good sized piece at a time. Dig your fire pit a good eight inches deep in the desert floor. Make it a foot wide and about two feet long. Since there is little humus or topsoil in many areas, you are already into mineral soil and there is little chance of fire spreading underground.

Pile up the loose mineral soil around the edges to make the hole deeper. Don't put stones around the fire pit. They get black and are dead giveaways from long distances. Break your burnables into various sizes to get the fire going. Then cook your meal, smoke your pipe, sip your brandy, or just dream by the fire. Enjoy. When you are done with the fire at night, let it burn out and douse it with water in the morning, after breakfast.

If you use a morning fire, follow these directions. If you are camped by available water, douse it until you can spread your hand through the coals and not get burned. If you have no water for dousing, you must put the coals out with dirt and give it the same hand test. Next, pulverize the coals and spread the powder in all directions to the wind if you are in a heavily vegetated area. (If not, then carry the powder in double plastic bags until you reach such an area. If you never reach this type of area, carry the ashes home.) Refill the fire pit with the soil, smooth it over and kick a couple of rocks onto it. Scatter the remaining burnables. Do not bury the coals; the next thunderstorm can unearth them and they will leave a black scar. Sound like a lot of trouble? Not if you plan the *time* for it just as you plan the time to cook the meal. Make it part of your time control plan.

Learn from this fiery tale: A girl friend and I were camping out in one of my favorite spots—a tributary of Tonto Creek near Payson, Arizona. We cooked steaks on a small grill over a small fire in a corner of a rock wall. When we were done with dinner I put the fire out with dirt (I thought). It was dark and the stream water located a tricky climb down a rock wall. We dozed off and a breeze came up. Marnie woke me with a scream. The breeze had fanned at least one remaining live coal into a flame that had jumped to my pack. The pack was aflame. I jumped up, grabbed the pack, and smothered it. The bottom compartment had burned up along with one shoulder strap. I spent a good hour putting the rest of the coals out with more dirt. I couldn't reach the water, because my flashlight was a charred blob. The only humorous remnant from the incident was that my Timex watch, with the band and crystal burned off and the face charred brown, was still running.

Now you know the importance of putting out a fire. How about the rest of the campsite? Before you leave, you must look around for visible evidence of your presence and . . .

Pack It Out—Patch It Up

By now you are probably tired of hearing it, but it bears repeating: Everything shows up on the desert. Everything preserves well in the dry climate. Cans and litter last lifetimes. Pick up every piece of paper, butts, foil, strings, and whatever else is out of place. Scatter meeting-place logs and dinner table rocks. Mark the spot on your map so that next time you come this way you can check it out. You may find that someone else has "discovered" your spot and has left it looking like a dump. Well, clean it up again. We've got to start somewhere. If you throw out some uneaten cooked food, break it up into small pieces and scatter it away from camp. The ants and rodents will usually take care of it.

Well, now you have your backpack stove in the kitchen and you are trying it out. You have taken it apart a couple of times to see how it works. You are cooking up some freeze-dried beef stroganoff and adding some fresh vegetables and wine. Not bad. You turn on the kitchen tap and add a bit more water and realize how easy it is to get water at home— simply turn on the faucet. But how about out there on the desert? No faucets out there. Perhaps you should ponder this most precious of commodities.

6

Water in the Desert

. . . There ain't much.

Water is life. Not a single living thing on this planet can survive without it, and that includes creatures that live in the desert. Desert-dwelling flora and fauna have had millions of years of practice getting along with precious little of that precious stuff. You haven't. You will have to learn how to plan your water supply, how to conserve it, and what to do if your best-laid plans go awry.

Water Is Survival

Before discussing our water plan, let's find out how the human body reacts to the various stresses of hot, dry climates. An exhaustive study of the effects of the desert environment on the activities of men was carried out from 1942 through 1945 by a group of scientists called the Rochester Desert Unit. The original investigations took place during desert army maneuvers in the great American deserts, as well as in research laboratories under very controlled conditions. The summaries of the work verify what most desert hikers and dwellers have learned from experience. Briefly, when the temperature of an environment is higher than the body's temperature of ninty-nine degrees, the body must compensate for the heat gain in order for its internal temperature to remain stable. If the interior temperature goes above ninty-nine degrees, the body develops a fever and may eventually lose its ability to function and die. In the desert environment, excessive heat is introduced to the body by direct radiated sunlight, by ground heat radiation and conduction, by wind convection, and by body metabolism during exercise. All these factors result in the need for a cooling system to maintain an even body temperature.

The human body's evaporative cooling system is the sweat glands. There are more than two million of these glands all over the body. When the body becomes overheated, these glands push water out to the skin surface. When the water evaporates, it cools the skin and the blood which brought the heat out from within the body. The resulting water loss through sweating must be replenished or dehydration will occur. There are no known acclimatizing or drug factors that will reduce this process. This evaporative factor alone allows man to exist in the desert.

The only two ways to stay hydrated are to continually consume water or to stop sweating. Sweating is not always noticeable. In a breeze, you may feel no water on your skin because it is evaporating as soon as it reaches the surface. But if the air temperature is higher than ninty-nine degrees, you are sweating, brother, you are sweating. Natural thirst reactions make us drink water to keep hydrated, but the studies show that in desert conditions, the thirst may be quenched before the total need of the body is satisfied.

Desert Water Wisdom

The amount of water you should carry with you into the desert depends on your body and how hard you expect to make it work. The average quantity needed for a summer hike is at least one gallon per person per day. Throw in another quart for good measure. In addition to the water bottles stashed in your pack, you may want to carry a canteen on your belt just for indulgence.

Forget the idea that you can ration water, and your body

A typical desert rat, complete with empty gallon jug to fill when she finds the water hole. Photo by Dave Ganci.

will reduce its need. It simply does not happen. You must replace the water you lose through perspiration. Drink as much as you want when you want it. You cannot fool your internal cooling mechanism. If you try to, you may start to feel the effects of thirst-induced irrationality. Your mind may get fuzzy and you may start making wrong decisions. Other symptoms of dehydration include "cottonmouth," when your saliva gets thick. Slowness and slurring of speech, a lazy feeling, a general reduction of efficiency, a heavy tiredness, dark urine, and dizziness can mean insufficient water intake. A lack of salt due to heavy perspiring is thought to be another cause of dehydration symptoms.

If you are heading for a planned campsite that has been marked as a spring or intermittent stream on the map, you must assume it is dry and carry enough water for the camp and the next day's hike. If you camp at a water source, fill your belly before leaving. Drink until you slosh. It may feel uncomfortable at first but it will be well worth it. Your stomach is simply another container and it puts you ahead of the game. No, this does not mean that you will sweat more, only that you may produce a bit more urine. But the benefit will outmeasure this inconvenience.

We have already talked about the merits of hiking in early morning and evening, leaving the midday for a siesta. This is especially helpful in summer temperatures when perspiration is at its heaviest. To conserve sweat, wear a wide-brimmed hat and perhaps a white bandana hanging down over your neck. Take a lesson from the Arabs. Wear loose-fitting, light-colored cotton clothing to reflect the radiated heat away from your body. Keep your foam pad or air mattress handy to sit on when taking a break. This will keep you off the superhot ground. Pull out that buried celery stick and chew on it while hiking. Don't overexert. Rest often in the shade. If you are running behind your time control plan, don't try to rush it in the heat of the day to make up time. Better to get to camp a little late than exhausted.

Your body will not need to cool off as much during the winter months, therefore your need for water will be reduced.

Take plenty anyway. Keep in mind that water weighs a little more than eight pounds per gallon, and while that will seem quite heavy in your pack, everything else in your pack will be worthless if you run out of it.

Water Caches

When you have graduated to the stage of extended desert treks, you may plan a cross-country route for which you cannot carry enough water, and where there is little chance of finding any. You may choose to cache water, food, film, or whatever, to be picked up as you travel along your proposed route. In your preplanning you will have picked out a campsite that is close to a roadhead from which you have carried the cache and deposited it ahead of time. Or perhaps you will make a foot trip along the route just to cache some water, then return to use it on your longer trip at a later date.

However you do it, keep in mind that you must be able to carry out all the containers along your route and leave no trace of your passing. Collapsible polyethylene containers are ideal since they are light to begin with and fold down for easy packing when empty. They usually come in one-, two-, or five-gallon sizes and can be bought in camping stores. Glass bottles are totally impractical.

When you bury your cache, wrap everything in at least two layers of extra-heavy plastic sheeting to help keep the water and food odor from attracting varmints. Bury the cache 18 inches underground and mark the spot with a pile of stones and dead saguaro or other cactus ribs. Be sure to mark the cache spot on your map.

There is a chance that water will freeze in cold climates, so do not fill your containers completely if you expect freezing temperatures along the route. Also, remember to pack the soil loosely, not tightly, around the containers to allow for possible expansion from freezing.

What happens if you reach the cache on the real trip and somebody has dug it up and taken it? Or animals have gotten to it and emptied the contents? Or an earthquake shook the area, broke the bottles, and the devil is just harassing you? In your time control plan, you should have made some contingency planning. When you arrive at a cache you must have enough water left on your person to make it to your next cache or back to your base camp. You can walk at night to conserve water if you don't mind a few cholla cacti jumping out at you. If you choose to move on to your next cache, make very sure you can pinpoint where you are at all times on the map. If you choose to return to camp, the same applies, but since you have been keeping track of landmarks along the route, it should not pose a difficult problem. I have hiked many a desert mile at night, under moonlight, bright starlight, and no light. Some night hikes have been pleasant experiences; during others, I think I would just as soon have been in Philadelphia. So the real answer, then, to how much water to take into the desert is more than you think you will need—just in case of emergencies. Keep track of how much you drink on each trip and adjust accordingly. But what about water on the desert?

Water, Water Anywhere?

If you have studied your maps, you have noted springs, wells, windmills, cattle tanks, old mines, intermittent and year-round streams, seeps, and caves. Identify these en route and see if there actually is water available. Enter the date and quantity of water in your notebook for future reference. You will find that water *is* available but very scarce. While water was exceedingly plentiful in these areas 30,000 or so years ago during the ice age, Nature has seen fit to withdraw her moisture sources over the course of time, leaving us with the lands of little water. Nevertheless, Nature is tricky and not always what she seems to be. There are hidden little nooks, crannies, potholes, canyon depths, tinajas, cliff edges, green areas, and other possible sources of the precious liquid. While hiking along, note steep gulleys and drainage areas. Do you spot an exceptionally green spot on the side of a hill? Investigate if you have planned the time. Look for bedrock gulleys where the overlying soil has weathered away. These

A tinaja, or natural water cache, in the White Tanks Mountains east of Phoenix, Arizona. The White Tanks are so named because of the white colored granite that forms basins to trap rainwater. Courtesy of Maricopa County Parks, Arizona.

often form shallow depressions for rainwater caches called tinajas. When you are traveling in hilly or mountainous terrain, stop every so often and look below with your field glasses. Do you see any reflections glaring back at you? Good chance of a pothole. Look for sycamores, cottonwoods, and seepwillows in dry streambeds. They stick out like green thumbs; a possible seep or spring here. After a rain, you may find numerous small potholes hiding in the corners of dry streambeds, camouflaged by underbrush. I've lived off of these for days in the Grand Canyon. I have strained the water through a T-shirt or I have sucked it up with a piece of rubber surgical tubing.

A rare occasion: a brief winter desert snow cover in the vicinity of a free-flowing desert stream. This is in Sabino Canyon, about 15 miles from Tucson.

Lavas and limestones tend to hold the most water and have the most springs. Limestone caves—any caves for that matter—may contain water seepage or even a spring. Green vegetation around the mouth of a cave is a sure sign of water somewhere. Look for water at the base of rock walls that cross lava flows. Often exposed sandstone canyon walls have seepages. You can spot the dark streaks dripping down the wall. Small, green mosses and leaves may be growing out of the streaks. Look along the bases of steep cliffs in mountainous areas. You may find water or a damp spot where water has been. You might dig down a short distance and allow some water to collect. Strain it through that clean T-shirt. Dry

Desert water holes are few and far between, for people and animals. Leave nothing but footprints behind. Photo by Dave Ganci.

streambeds may also have underground water along the inside curves. Dig down, and if you hit wet sand, you may find water farther down.

Windmill tanks often contain water, even if the structure hasn't been tended for years. It would be wise to purify this water, and any other water found in tanks or cattle ponds. If you are in doubt about a water source, purify it in any one of the following ways:

1. Boil for at least 1 minute.
2. Drop iodine tablets in a quart of water; shake, and let stand 15 minutes. Or place 8 drops of 2.5 percent iodine solution in same.
3. Place 1 Halazone tablet in a pint of water; let it stand thirty minutes after the tablet has dissolved.
4. Add 16 drops of fresh household bleach to a quart of water; let it stand 10 minutes.

There is no substitute for personal experience and the knowledge you gain from each excursion into the desert. At first, this dry land may seem inhospitable—harsh, hard, brown, sharp, craggy, sticky. But as you get to know the desert, you will learn the little secrets of being comfortable there. You will learn that water is out there in closely guarded places. You will learn that you can even get water from the sun.

Water from the Sun

A solar still is an emergency device by which water is evaporated from the earth or from cut up vegetation. It is then condensed back onto a piece of plastic that allows it to drip into a pot. The components of the still include a six-foot square or circular piece of Tedlar plastic sheeting, a two- to four-quart container with a wide mouth, an eight-foot piece of surgical tubing, and a digging tool such as a trowel or sharp rock.

The principle of operation is that solar energy passes

through the plastic and is absorbed by the soil, resulting in evaporation of water, followed by condensed water that runs down to the point of the cone and drops into the container, from which it is collected (see diagram). The still is constructed by digging a round hole about 18 inches deep and 40 inches across. The center is dug out deeper to accommodate the container. Tape the plastic tubing to the container with the other end coming out of the hole and available to drink from. The plastic cover is put over the hole and held in place around the edge with soil. The plastic is then pushed downward in the center to form a cone having an angle of twenty-five to forty degrees. A rock is placed in the center over the container to maintain the conical shape. More soil is placed around the edges to hold the plastic in place. The plastic sheet should be about six inches above the soil inside the hole and should touch the soil only on the rim. It usually takes from one to two hours for any visible condensation to start. Depending on the soil conditions, a solar still may yield from one to three pints of water per day. If the soil is very dry, you can add cut-up plant material—saguaro, prickly pear, and barrel cactus—to the inside walls of the hole to increase the yield. Do not let the cacti touch the plastic.

The location of the still depends on availability of cacti and the softness of the soil. If you are in an area with no water-holding plants, some soil is better than others. Generally, a clay soil is better than sand because it holds more water longer. But wet sand in a streambed is ideal.

You would realistically need two or three stills to sustain you in any long-term survival situation. I have never known anyone who has actually had to survive with one, but you might experiment with it in your backyard.

My first desert survival situation occurred in my younger days when the Gods of Youth somehow give us a little extra strength to tide us through our stupidities. Rick Tidrick, an early climbing companion, and I made a climb of an untrod-upon sandstone temple in the middle of the Grand Canyon. Our last water stop was to be at Bright Angel Creek by Phantom Ranch. We would cover a distance of 5,000 vertical feet over a horizontal distance of five miles—the last 600 feet being a sandstone rock climb. We waited in Phoenix until rain was forecast for the canyon. It was late September. When we got word that it was raining on the rim, we were off. By the time we got there, the rains had stopped, but clouds swirled around the temples. We spent the night at Phantom Ranch and headed up onto the Tonto Plateau, carrying two gallons of water plus a five-gallon metal jerry can to catch water in when it rained again. We found a route up the 500-foot Red Wall limestone in the inner canyon, and reached the top that night—hauling our clanking jerry can with us. We set it up with a plastic tarp to funnel in the rain water from the predicted storm. We waited two days for rain, hauling our climbing gear up to the base and retreating back to our camp in hopes of drinking the collected rainfall. No rain. We could wait no longer and went back up to do the climb. It took us two days. We had one gallon of water between us, plus the remains of two water pockets filled with creepy crawlies that we strained through our teeth. We bivouaced on the temple. In the middle of the night, delirious, I grabbed the canteen, intent on finishing it. Rick grabbed it out of my hand and shook me awake. I had been dreaming of dying of thirst. We finished the climb the next day, rapelled off the temple in a fuzzy daze, and returned to camp. Still no rain. Next day, we stumbled down the Red Wall to the Tonto Plateau and were inundated with a cloudburst. We stopped at every water pocket on the way to Phantom Ranch. We lost fifteen pounds each. Another day or two without water would have done us in.

Things have come a long way since the jerry can days, but neither the canyon nor the dehydration principles has changed. The water pockets we had found, high in the inner canyon, were our salvation.

7

Desert First Aid and Survival Plan

. . . If it hurts, rub a toad on it. (Max Davison)

I think most outdoor books recommend the carrying of too much first aid and emergency gear. You cannot possibly cover all the bases. About every month a new emergency gadget appears on the market to make you feel safer in the wilderness. To me the prime example of this is the snakebite kit. I have sold literally millions of these while in business, and millions more are stuck away in first aid pouches. I have never known anyone who has ever used one—or for that matter *would* use one—in the event of a snakebite. To me their value is strictly psychological.

The point I am trying to make here is that there are only a few medical situations that you will be able to handle anyway unless you are a trained paramedic, nurse, or physician. If you encounter broken bones, bad burns, severe cuts, serious head injuries, internal injuries, or back and neck injuries, there is little you can do other than immobilize the victim, clean and cover the wounds, stop the bleeding, and treat for shock until you can get the victim professional medical help. Still, you should know how to do these things properly, especially the last one, treating for shock. Take basic and advanced first aid

courses from your local Red Cross. Emergency medical techni-
cian courses are also sometimes available at community
colleges. Buy a good first-aid book (see the Appendix for
recommendations) and study it thoroughly.

Common Complaints and Treatments

The most frequent desert hiking affliction is the blister. We
have discussed boot fit and break-in time. But even if your
boots are fairly broken in, your feet may not be in shape for
that overnighter. Put adhesive tape around the backs of both
heels before you trek out. Take some foot powder, rubbing
alcohol, and Moleskin. If a painful blister forms, prick the
bottom of the swelling with a sterile needle and drain it. Then
cover it with a bandage and a layer of adhesive tape. You can
let it dry and heal when you get back to camp or when you
get home.

Take care of your feet during the day's hike. When you stop
for a rest, take off your boots, shake out your socks, and rub
your feet with a little alcohol. If you feel a blister forming,
put some adhesive tape over it right then. Keep toenails
cleaned and trimmed. Use foot powder. Keep those tootsies in
shape. They get you there and bring you back. Be kind to
them; their vengeance can put you back in the armchair.

The second most common complaint I have observed while
trodding the deserts is spines, spikes, and needles embedded in
the epidermis of howling hikers. Cacti love people and beckon
them—almost dare them—to touch and see if their stickers
really are sharp. Sometimes you can be five feet away from
that cholla and still pick up stickers from an unseen stem that
lies brown and hidden on the ground. Zap! Right through
those tough leather boots. A simple pocket comb can remove
most hangers-on. You will need a pair of tweezers and
sometimes a magnifying glass to get those teeny tiny, hair-
sized stickers out of your fingers. I will bet you the price of
this book that you get a finger-full the first time you pick a
prickly pear fruit.

Minor burns are best treated by covering the affected area

with cold water. Forget ointment, butter, or toad juice. Serious burns require evacuation and a physician's care.

Stomach and intestinal disorders may be brought on by freeze-dried foods or by the simple disruption of your normal dietary habits, especially if you have a sensitive digestive tract. The general shock of a completely new environment can stop you up for a couple days. These annoying inconveniences will be less likely to occur as you get out more often.

Heat-Related Ailments
The human body, as amazing as it is, can survive only within the narrow limits of a certain temperature and chemical balance. Extreme heat or cold can upset that balance and cause problems. Desert heat problems are usually of two kinds: (1) Direct and reflected sunlight on the skin that causes sunburns and sunblindness; and (2) Dehydration problems resulting in heat stroke, heat exhaustion, and heat cramps. These overlap, but we will discuss them separately.

Insufficient water intake, overexertion, and overheating can lead to heat stroke, a major emergency. The symptoms are:

1. Red face
2. Headache and nausea
3. Hot, dry skin due to the breakdown of the sweating process
4. Strong and rapid pulse
5. High fever
6. Unconsciousness and possibly convulsions

The first aid treatment for sunstroke is:

1. Move victim to shady spot
2. Lay victim back with head and shoulders slightly above body
3. Cool victim any way possible—applying wet towels, dampening clothing, fanning, applying ice
4. Withhold stimulants
5. Give lightly salted water in sips
6. Get victim to medical aid

Heat exhaustion is not as serious as heat stroke, but can develop rapidly into serious trouble. The symptoms are:

1. Nausea, weakness, dizziness, and vomiting
2. Normal temperature
3. Weak pulse
4. Cool, clammy, moist body
5. Pale face
6. Fainting

First aid treatment for heat exhaustion is:

1. Move victim to shady spot
2. Lay victim down and loosen clothing
3. Give lightly salted water every 15 minutes
4. Get victim to medical aid

Heat cramps occur when too much salt is lost from the body through perspiration. Your muscles tighten and the pain is intense. Water and salt intake will usually relieve them.

As always, the best medicine is preventive medicine, and since heat can be a constant companion on the desert, follow the common sense rules we discussed in Chapter 6.

The Cold Can Get You Too

Hypothermia and frostbite are serious matters and can occur in cold desert winters, especially at night. The combination of falling temperatures, precipitation, and wind can change a pleasant shirt-sleeve day into a deadly night for the unprepared. Your climate control plan should account for these situations.

Hypothermia occurs when the body's core temperature drops below ninety-five degrees Fahrenheit. When the body becomes cold, blood tries to keep the vital organs warmer. The legs, arms, feet, and hands are chilled and soon the whole body chills. The symptoms are shivering, confusion, difficulty in speech, slowed reactions, loss of judgment. Warm the victim by every means possible—warm bottles, warm bodies, clothing, sleeping bags, fires, and warm drinks. Get the person to medical aid.

Frostbite is the freezing of an exposed part of the body. Mild frostbite is characterized by numbness, and cold, blanched skin. It will go away, perhaps rather painfully, with adequate and prompt warming. The flesh may redden and blister. Deep frostbite causes a total numbness and rigidity. Waxy, blanched skin is characteristic. The victim must be evacuated.

Creepy Crawlies
New desert insect varieties are being discovered yearly. Thousands of species have been identified. For some reason, some men and almost all women—sorry, but it's true—have fears of insects that are all out of proportion to these critters' ability to do them harm. Very few insects purposely seek out man in order to harass him. Mosquitoes, flies, ants, gnats, some ticks, and a few no-see-ems are the exception. But 99.9 percent of all insects are just doing business as usual when man intervenes in their environment. Insects seem to be continually building, hunting, eating, chasing—busy all the time. They are adapted for survival in thousands of subtle ways. They are fantastic machines of unending variety and the lowest visible element of life's food chain. Many birds, mammals, and plants would simply cease to exist without the insects as food, pollinators, and aerators of the soil. An unnatural fear of insects is usually based on ignorance or misinformation. Perhaps by reading and learning the facts about insects, people will eventually be able to replace their fear of insects with a healthy respect for them and the important role they play in the environment.

A typical example of ignorance and misinformation concerning insects is the tarantula, a large, furry spider that has sparked the imagination of sensation seekers everywhere. Tarantulas live in underground homes, coming out in the evenings to hunt, socialize, and mate. Knowledgeable children have made pets of them, allowing them to crawl up and down arms and legs. Sure, if you molest them they are going to nip you, just like any other critter. They are part of the system and are simply doing their job. If you lay your ground cloth next to one of their holes, you can bet they will investigate. That is no reason to stomp them. Simply move your camp.

I have seen more scorpions in old houses than on the desert. They are out there, to be sure, but they are hard to find. Again, they have nothing against you unless you disturb them. They like to hang around lumber, logs, dead cactus limbs, old dwellings, and machinery. If you happen to get stung by one, keep your cool. Well, kill the scorpion first, then keep your cool. There are only a couple of potent scorpions and they are rare. But you might want to take the culprit with you for identification if you suffer a strong reaction. Treat the affected area with ice or cold water as soon as possible to slow down the reaction. Everyone reacts differently to insect bites, due to personal chemical makeup. Some people suffer only a mild soreness that goes away in a day; others suffer heavy swelling and nausea. There is also the possibility of delayed reactions, so my advice is to end the trek and see a doctor.

This same advice applies to black widow spider bites. But these, too, are extremely rare. In fact, statistically, more folks suffer bad reactions from bee stings than from scorpion or black widow bites.

Centipedes and giant millipedes are relatively harmless. True, they are ugly, but leave them alone. They have their purpose in the food chain, and to put things in proper perspective, their ancestors were around long before ours.

Remember, there are no good guys or bad guys in the insect world. They are all just trying to make a living. Admire their tenacity in the face of tremendous odds. For instance, one bat can eat hundreds of winged ants in a night's hunting. A nighthawk can devour 500 mosquitoes the same night. Hmmm . . . perhaps I will make a pet out of a nighthawk for those mosquito-filled Sierra evenings.

The Big Bad Rattler

At least 12 species of rattlesnakes inhabit the western deserts. The largest and most dangerous is the western diamondback.

Lucky is the hiker who spots one, since they are quite rare. Like all snakes of the desert, the diamondback stays underground or coiled around bushes and hedges in the summer daytime, coming out in the evening hours to hunt and socialize. In cooler desert areas, the rattlers hibernate all winter. Snakes are often spotted stretched out on the road pavement on cool evenings. They soak up the pavement heat this way.

Rattlesnakes are pit vipers possessing heat-sensing mechanisms to detect other animals at considerable distance. These pits, located between the eyes and nostrils, pick up heat radiations that the snake follows until it comes within striking distance of the object. When the rattler is close enough to the dinner of his choice, he strikes quickly, injects his venom, then lets go. The victim dies quickly, whereupon the rattler dines at his leisure. His fare includes insects, frogs, mice, and young birds. He in turn is on the menus of roadrunners, owls, and hawks. Man is not part of the rattler's diet. The rattler does not seek man; he defends his territory against man's intrusion.

Documented histories of rattlesnake bites compiled by the Arizona Game and Fish Department show that 90 percent of all bites occur while the person is antagonizing the snake. There are more recorded deaths by lightning than by rattlers.

Many people recommend high-top boots for desert hiking, solely on the basis of protection against snakebite. I do not. High-top boots constrict calves and tendons and are hotter than low-cuts. The chances of getting bitten are extremely remote, and there is little evidence that a rattler's fangs cannot penetrate leather anyway. Chances are, you will hear a rattler before you will see one. The sound is unforgettable.

But what to do if you are that one in a million who gets nailed. Don't try to capture the snake. You risk a repeat performance. You'll know it is a rattler by his rattles.

One-third of rattlesnake bites are 'dry' bites—bites injecting no venom. Venomous bites will induce immediate burning and usually swelling. First aid for snakebite begins with getting the victim to calm down, whether the victim is yourself or someone else.

Unless you have been trained, forget about making incisions. Just put suction cups on, if they are available. If not, you can try sucking out the venom with your mouth. Do not try to administer antivenin unless you are trained.

Next, immobilize the injured part with a splint or a sling. The patient should sit or lie down. Attempt to evacuate by litter or other transportation. If the patient must walk, walk him slowly and rest often. Do not exert! If possible, get emergency rescue service.

Keep a record of the treatment. Note the time and date of the bite. Note the kind of snake if possible—its color, size, rattles, head shape. Note pulse and keep track of shock symptoms. All this is invaluable to a physician when he receives the patient.

As far as I know, there have been no controlled, scientific experiments testing a victim's reactions to rattlesnake poison—for obvious reasons. Therefore, there has been great conjecture and disagreement concerning emergency treatment. The above is about the best you can do without medical training.

Anyway, there I was, surrounded by rattlers in a remote canyon near the Village of Supai—the land of blue-green waters—located in Havasu Canyon on the west end of the Grand Canyon. It was night, and I was looking for an access up and out of the canyon to the Esplanade flat land above. I heard one rattle—then another, and another. I was in the middle of what sounded like a hundred rattlers (probably five or six). Even though my total awareness multiplied by ten, I could not see them. I wanted to throw up. I turned around very slowly and made some even slower night moves. I tiptoed so high I was actually walking on the ends of my boots. Fight or flight—the old midbrain took over and I flew out of the canyon. I was lucky. No, I was stupid. I was both. I shouldn't have been hiking in that ink-black canyon at night, in the fall. It was the only time in thousands of hiking hours that I was ever threatened by any kind of wildlife, and that was only because I stepped into their evening meeting uninvited. I will knock first next time.

Evacuation

One of the hardest decisions to make in a medical emergency is whether to evacuate a victim or to leave the victim and bring medical aid to the site. This situation requires a cool, reasoned approach and the weighing of several factors:

1. The nature of the injury and the terrain over which you must travel while evacuating the victim
2. The number of people who can help carry the victim
3. The time of day
4. The weather, including temperature considerations
5. The amount of equipment and supplies on hand
6. The energy and experience levels of other members in the group
7. The distance to help or to communications points, such as roadheads, from which you can call for help

All of these factors are variable, just as emergency situations are variable. Good judgment is the key. And what is good judgment? In this case, it is the ability to relate a specific circumstance to the big picture. Panic, the opposite of judgment, is the immediate reaction to the specific circumstance. Fight or flight is panic. You must exercise judgment by sitting down and formulating a plan.

After you have given first aid and made the victim comfortable, psychologically as well as physically, get everyone together to discuss the situation. Let everyone know right away that you will make the final decision to evacuate the victim or to go for help. Take charge. Delegate responsibilities among the group. Keep everyone busy. Now, will the long range safety of the victim—and the safety of those evacuating—be served by taking the victim out? Or is there a better chance of quick rescue if someone is sent out for help?

While you are weighing all the factors, keep *written* notes. You are playing the odds, so know what the odds are. You cannot possibly keep all of the factors in mind while under duress. If you write all the factors down, you will probably choose a course of action with the odds in your favor. The record you have kept of the victim's accident, treatment, and response will help.

If you decide to send for outside help, put all the instructions to the would-be rescuers in writing also. No exceptions! You know how communications can get fouled up. Compound that by the emergency factor, and you may compound the seriousness of the situation. If you decide to send a runner, try to send two just in case one runs into his own emergency. Send the written instructions on a map that shows the route you have taken and the exact spot where you will be located. Tell the rescuers what to look for should they come in by air. Examples are sleeping bags spread out, "HELP" banners, and fires.

Remember that those going for help have to survive also. Do you have enough water to remain while waiting for the rescue? How much will the runners have to take? Will they have to spend a night out before reaching help? Is there water available along the way? Since you have made a time and distance control plan as part of your pretrip thinking, everything about the route should be pretty well spelled out on your map already.

If the decision is to evacuate a victim who either cannot or should not walk on his own, a makeshift litter can be made from materials at hand: pack frames, ropes, saguaro ribs, tree limbs, anything you can find. Litter construction details are discussed in the books recommended in the Appendix.

Getting Lost

Let's say that you are out hiking one day and about midafternoon you look at your map. It says you should be at a spring but there's no spring in sight. Your map tells you that you should see a sheer cliff straight ahead. Oh-oh, no cliff either. You realize you are completely turned around and all the landmarks look different. You sit down, make a calm estimate of the situation and conclude that you are lost.

Well, maybe you are and maybe you aren't. Don't let that first feeling of panic and disorientation throw you. You may be *temporarily* lost, a phenomenon that sometimes occurs in the wilderness. You may have been thinking about a story or a photograph, or just plain daydreaming for a mile or so, when suddenly you realize that you have not kept track of where you are headed. Time to sit down, study the map, and pinpoint the spot where you last remember you *weren't* lost. Look back over the terrain and try to find a prominent landmark. Set your pack down and go up the nearest hill, keeping your pack in view, and get a bird's-eye view of the topography. Does that cliff ring a bell? How about that streambed? That canyon? Did you pass them a while ago when you were daydreaming? How about that abandoned Jeep trail shown on the map? Ah, wait a minute! There it is. The Jeep trail. And that cliff is visible back about a half mile. The spring must be that green area with the cottonwoods sticking up. Your route was supposed to cross that Jeep track about a quarter mile back. Okay, all the directions make sense on the map now. You go back and get yourself on trail again and decide to save the dreaming for the campfire.

But what about the situation in which you discover that you really *are* lost, and it's about one hour until sundown, and you were out on a day hike with no provisions for an overnight camp. What to do?

First of all, sit down and relax until that first rush of panic subsides. Then try to forget about tomorrow and the fact that you are lost. You must concentrate on making camp for the night. This will give you a chance to use all your ingenuity. Consider it a challenge, not a threat. Look for a spot that offers some shelter, maybe some cliff ledges or a clump of mesquite trees. Gather firewood while it is still light. Set up a windbreak with stones. Consider a heat reflective wall such as a stack of stones, a cliff wall, a tube tent, or tarp. Soften up the ground with a sharp rock or your boot heel. This will be your mattress. Get all your firewood stacked by your bed and within reach of the fire pit. Eat up your remaining snacks and take stock of your water situation. Don't save it until morning if you are thirsty that night. Be prepared for a few irrational fears of darkness, animals, and boogie men. This is all part of the psychological response to the unknown. Recognize them for what they are and ignore them. Slip your pack over your feet and lower legs. Make note of where the sun goes down, and then guess just about where it will come up at dawn. You will want to catch the rays as soon as possible after your chilly bivouac. Many people have survived extremely cold nights on forced bivouacs. You will too. You may not be comfortable and you may not get much sleep. But you'll be in good enough shape to make your return trip or set up a temporary camp the next day.

All right, it's morning and you are cold and stiff. Get that fire going strong to warm up the bones. Revel in the new day and warming rays of the sun. You reflect a bit on that small rock rat that kept you company most of the night, nibbling on cheese crumbs. You laugh when you remember how adapted he is to his environment—heavy fur coat, warm underground home, food supply all around, water somewhere. He can live out there indefinitely. But you can't. So take stock of the situation and climb up that nearby hill. Again, look for prominent landmarks that you can identify on the map. If you don't find any, then you must decide if you are going to try to find your way back or make a camp and wait for a rescue. You know the general direction you came from and the general direction you were headed when you discovered you were lost. Since your proposed route is marked on the map, you can retrace the previous afternoon's steps until you can identify a landmark circled on the map. Then you should be able to reorient yourself and either head back to camp or continue on the route.

If you don't find that landmark in about an hour, and you still don't know where you are, it's time for the next course of action. How much water do you have with you? If you stop right where you are and make camp, is there enough water to hold you until the rescue party has had time to search? How many more days until they actually will start looking for you? Add at least another two days until they spot your fires and signals up on top of that hill. If your water supply is limited you must search for water as you keep on heading back toward what you think is your return route. This way you may suddenly recognize a landmark and become oriented again. At any rate, you will need water, so apply the information in Chapter 6. Do your traveling in the early morning and late afternoon to conserve perspiration. Each time before you head out, climb to a high point and pick out a destination, at the same time scouring the horizon for a landmark and reflections of possible water pockets. Try to pick a streambed to follow. You may find small water pockets tucked away in one corner that you would otherwise miss.

If you find a good water source, consider making camp and waiting for rescue. Set up visible signals on a high point. Gather plenty of firewood. You may wish to make your camp on the high point, keeping your warming fire going all night, thereby also making it visible all night. Try to keep it going all day. When the time has arrived for the rescuers to start looking for you, have some green plants around to put on the fire. These will create black smoke that can be seen for long distances. Carry a signal mirror as part of your emergency kit.

If it will be days until the rescue is scheduled, you may wish to take short day hikes away from your watered camp to try and get reoriented. Just don't get more lost. Set up markers every quarter mile or so. Try to keep the camp within visible distance.

You have your first-aid kit, which will take care of most superficial medical problems. You decide you might want to add a few items in case you get stuck out again. Consider the following:

1. Thermal blanket—lightweight, compact, reflective.
2. Brass whistle—a good call for help.
3. More nylon cord—always comes in handy.
4. Disposable butane lighter—wet matches are useless.
5. A second small flashlight—the first one will always go out on you—Murphy's law.
6. More tea bags—tea cheers you up.
7. Vest or wool sweater—I know you don't need it during the day.
8. A better book to read—*Alive* is not the one when you are bivouacing.

You've been on a number of lowland desert hikes now, and you want a change of pace. You've been eyeing those desert mountains that make themselves so conspicious, sticking up out of the desert floor. Why not? You can get a taste of as many as seven more different life zones by expanding your horizons upward. You can go from the Lower Sonoran desert up through the Upper Sonoran, grassland, pinyon-juniper woodland, oak woodland, oak-pine woodland, ponderosa pine forest, and even the Douglas fir forest in one good weekend backpack. That is equivalent to traveling 3,000 miles north-ward into Canada. These *mini* life zones exist as part of the vertical topography of many desert mountain chains. As a matter of fact, a whole book could be written on desert mountains—their trails and topography!

For right now, however, I will give you a brief introduction as to what to expect when you venture upward into . . .

8

Desert Mountains

. . . Dust storm, hell—that's snow!

The deserts are still geologically young. Desert peaks and mountains show their youth by their jagged, sharp, jutting crests. The sparseness of vegetation gives the gaunt look to desert ridges. Bare rock is everywhere, and in the summertime the rocks absorb so much heat that you may not even want to touch them. The desert peaks have presence, and draw many climbers, backpackers, and day hikers up their slopes with the promise of a 100-mile, 360-degree view of the surrounding lands.

Basically, any upward-jutting prominence covered with desert vegetation is a desert peak. These peaks are not high enough above the desert floor to have a different climatic zone. But they are high enough to catch desert winds, and they extend into the Upper Sonoran Desert life zone. Thousands of these isolated peaks jut up in solitary vigil over the sweeping valley floors. Others form long, narrow ranges, the silhouettes of which capture the eye and camera lens for untold numbers of sunset hours. Many of these peaks can be climbed in a day from their base, with a lunchtime view from their summit.

117

The trailhead at Squaw Peak City Park in Phoenix. This park is part of the Phoenix Mountains Preserve, a unique desert recreation area in the middle of Phoenix. Photo by Dave Ganci.

Some have trails, thousands more do not. They require scrambling. It is a good idea to know what to expect.

If you think some of the desert foliage is unfriendly on the flatlands, you will think they are downright hostile on desert peaks. The problem, of course, is not that the plants are any more numerous, but that we are more off balance and not always as selective about where we put our feet down.

Rough and tricky terrain challenges the uphill push. Since

rainfall is slight, binding soil is scarce and rocks that appear secure can crumble and pull off when you step on them or grab on with your hands. Decomposed granite can feel like marbles under your feet and put you in the prone position pronto.

Dehydration dangers become even greater if you scramble up a desert peak. You are exerting more, sweating more, and the winds are absorbing and evaporating more perspiration at a faster rate than when you are tramping on the flatlands. You must carry *at least* a gallon plus a quart of water on full-day climbs. The exposure to wind, and even brighter sunlight, can dry your skin quickly and cause chapped lips and sunburn in a hurry.

Many times there is no road access to a desert peak. The approach would normally require an off-road vehicle. If you believe as I do that off-road vehicles have no place in the desert except on roads, you will have to make your approach from the nearest roadhead. And why not? That makes the peak an even greater challenge.

Be sure to take along a pair of binoculars for the view from the top. A local Phoenix climbing group, the Arizona Mountaineering Club, holds annual kite-flying days off the tops of local desert peaks. Your advantageous perch affords a hawk's-eye view of wildlife, It also gives you a chance to spot those reflecting water potholes, just in case you need them.

Those highlands that stretch beyond the Upper Sonoran Desert and extend from the grassland up to the ponderosa pine and Douglas fir forests are sometimes referred to as desert mountain islands. The higher ones offer a variety of plant, animal, and climate zones that appear nowhere else on earth in so small an area. Some of these islands are located where you could pass through most of these zones in a long day hike. Others require multiday backpacks.

One such range of desert mountains forms the northern backdrop of the second largest city in Arizona, Tucson. Called the Santa Catalinas, these mountains form a dramatic skyline that terminates at the summit of Mt. Lemmon, 9,157 feet

The top of Squaw Peak with views of the local desert mountain chain in the background. Photo by Dave Ganci.

above sea level. Since Tucson receives almost 20 inches of rain a year, the surrounding desert is lush and beautiful. Hikers can go from this Upper Sonoran life zone all the way up to the Douglas fir stands at the crest. More than 170 miles of trails crisscross the 200-square-mile range. There is an observatory on the summit of Mt. Lemmon and the country's southernmost winter ski area drops off the ridgeline.

With more than 6,000 feet of elevation gain and many

horizontal miles of trails, it is easy to see that many different climatic situations can exist for the hiker. Summertime temperatures can rise above 100 degrees Fahrenheit as high as 6,000 feet above sea level on the mountain; snow can be several feet deep with subzero temperatures in the higher parts of the range during the winter. Local hikers usually frequent the higher elevations in the hot months and enjoy the lower trails in the cold season.

Except for the snow, water is still scarce in these islands. You must carry enough to last you the entire hike, unless you are familiar with the area and know where to locate water. You should carry extra-warm clothing for the cooler, windier elevations. Take a lightweight down jacket, even on a day hike. Take extra food. You will be exerting more and using more calories than when hiking on the valley floor.

Time and again, hikers get into trouble when they first experience the mountains. They tend to overestimate their abilities and underestimate the distances and ruggedness of the hills. The same distance deception takes place in the mountains as in the desert flatlands. Many hikers get lost or disoriented in the mountains if they stray off trail. Ridges start looking alike, and if you are not following a time and distance control plan, and sticking with your maps, it is not hard to get turned around. Know what canyon you are in. Know what streambed you are crossing. Know what that ridge is up ahead; pick it out on your map. Know that it will take you two to three times as long to reach a destination going uphill as it does on the straight and level. Don't plan a day hike that will get you back to your car at sundown. Plan at least a 10 percent hedge and get in an hour before sundown. If you find yourself behind your time and distance plan by midmorning, shorten the overall hike. You don't want to get caught out on a narrow, sparse trail in look-alike mountain country at night. Those cold canyons can make you feel mighty lonesome until morning. Study local trail guides and heed their warnings.

9

Desert Hiking and Camping Techniques

. . . Whaddaya mean, we're not bringing any toilet paper?

So far we have talked about making plans, about your vehicle, about water, survival, clothing and gear, food, first-aid, and mountains. So let's put it all together and plan an actual trip. Let's say you have been on a few day hikes, and you took a special interest course on backpacking at your local junior college that included one overnight trip. You have read this book and some of the others listed in the Appendix. You've decided you want to make backpacking a family affair, so you are going to take your spouse, son and daughter on a three-day trek into the Superstition Wilderness, thirty miles east of Phoenix, Arizona. It is springtime in the Lower Sonoran Desert, and you want to get out into it. It has been raining for the past two days, but now is clearing up. The forecast is for clear skies and warm temperatures. And everyone knows what the weather bureau means when they say warm. They mean hot during the day. The rain will have filled all the water pockets in the streambeds, and water should be easy to find.

You've gotten everyone outfitted now, and the final planning session before leaving for the trailhead is underway.

Since this will be the first overnight trip for the rest of your family, you want to have a discussion with them about planning.

Kes Teter and I were trudging up a slope on Mt. Fremont—a sister peak to Mt. Humphreys just north of Flagstaff, Arizona. It was October and the temperatures were mild. We got a late start, and planned to set up camp on the first flat spot we found. We were hiking in shorts and light shirts. The sun went down and we still hadn't found a flat spot. We reached the ridgeline at 9:30 P.M. and the wind hit us. It was pitch black, and we hadn't noticed the clouds moving in. The weather forecast had been for continued mild temperatures, with a possible front arriving a couple of days later. It was still fall on the peaks—until we started moving up the ridgeline. Snow flurries swirled around us, and we were soon in a whiteout. We changed into our long pants and wool shirts. At 10:30 P.M. we came to the first flat spot. It was a circle of rocks with a spot just big enough for our summer tent. It sloped off on the other side. It was the summit of Mt. Fremont. We pitched the tent in a blizzard and snuggled in. The snow piled up around the tent, and we had to continually push it off. A summer tent does not pitch as tight as a good mountain tent, and heavy snow will push in the sides and eventually collapse it.

We slept fitfully and finally dozed off for a few hours before dawn. When we awoke, our sleeping bags were covered with about eight inches of snow and there was a three-foot drift inside the doorway. We plowed our way out and peered around. The storm had subsided and everything was white; it had been green the day before. The first storm of the season had dumped on us. We had climbed up the mountain in the fall and were going back down in the winter. That's the way it can be in mountain country.

Planning

Your family is gathered around the kitchen table, and you all have copies of the Goldfield and Weaver's Needle USGS topographic maps. You are pointing the route out to your family and marking the trail with an orange felt-tip pen, circling the campsites. Base camp will be at Peralta Campground. You will car-camp there Thursday night and be ready to start up the trail at around 7:30 A.M. Friday morning.

You explain the time and distance control plan. It is about eight measured miles between base camp and your first overnight spot at Aylor's Camp. You throw in another half mile for those hard-to-measure switchbacks on the map. With 30-pound packs on your backs, you figure you can average close to 2 miles per hour with a 5-to 10-minute break every hour. So far, that's 4 hours and 15 minutes hiking time. Now, you check the elevation gain and loss. Peralta Campground is at 2,400 feet above sea level. Fremont Saddle, the highest point on the first day's hike, is at 3,766 feet, about a third of the distance to Aylor's Camp. You will be climbing 1,400 feet of elevation in the first two and a half miles, therefore you must add about another forty-five minutes to the time schedule for that uphill slog. From Fremont Saddle, you will descend gradually to Aylor's Camp at 2,300 feet elevation. If you plan on stopping at Fremont Saddle to enjoy the view, take photographs, eat some snacks, and just relax a bit, add another half hour to the total travel time. This adds up to five hours and thirty minutes from the time you leave Peralta. If you start at 7:30, you should mosey into Aylor's Camp, at about 1:00 P.M. Good! That's plenty of time on the trail for the first day out since packs will be heavy and feet will be getting used to the new hardships. Besides, you want plenty of time to set up shelters and talk about camping procedures. This will also ensure time to search for waterholes, gather some firewood, enjoy the wild flowers, and get your feet rubbed.

Now you and the family repackage all the food into double plastic bags which you mark for easy identification with a grease pencil. You recheck all the gear and stuff in an extra orange and chocolate bar. You make sure you have included the copy of Dr. Michael Sheridan's *Superstition Wilderness Guidebook*, 3rd ed. Tempe, Arizona: University of Arizona, 1975, and David Mazel's *Arizona Trails* (Wilderness Press, 1981), paperbacks on cacti and wild flowers that you purchased at the Desert Botanical Garden, and the pocket guides to desert mammals, birds, and insects that you borrowed.

You leave a map with the route marked on it with your next-door neighbor. The estimated time of arrival home is Sunday night about 8:00 P.M. Your neighbor knows that if you don't contact him by 8:00 P.M. Monday night, he should initiate a search with the help of the county sheriff's office.

The Campground

It's Thursday afternoon and all the packs are in the station wagon, along with the two spare tires and the rest of the survival gear. There is no water at Peralta Campground, so containers must be filled at home. There will be no firewood at Peralta either, so some must be picked up at the nursery on the way out of town.

Arriving at Peralta around 5:00 P.M., you set up camp, grill some steaks over the fire, cook up some beans, corn, and homemade bread and watch the colored light show put on by the desert sunset.

You sense the excitement of your family now, as they realize they are away from the crowds of civilization and are beginning to feel the kinship of the one-on-one relationship with the natural world. It's into the sleeping bags as the campfire embers die.

You rise at dawn to cook eggs and sausage on the two-burner car-camping stove. The fire is doused and the coals dumped into a plastic garbage bag to be hauled home. The unused firewood is collected for the next car camp. The cool morning dictates long pants and wool sweaters. The maps are folded and put in the plastic map holders. These are placed into the pockets sewn onto the pack shoulder straps for easy access.

The Trailhead

Up with the packs and off to the trailhead 100 yards up the road. It's close to 7:30 A.M. and you are off to a good start. At

At trailheads the map is oriented to the terrain features. Time and distance can be estimated here. Photo by Dave Ganci.

the trailhead you orient the maps to the terrain features: Ah, yes, the sun is rising in the east; the sheer Dacite Cliffs are on your left, or west, and the Peralta Canyon trail angles up northwest through Peralta Canyon to Fremont Saddle. The map also tells you that the brown, wavy contour lines are 40 vertical feet apart and marked off on the map at elevations of every 100 feet. All the contour lines crossing Peralta Canyon form ∧s, pointing upstream. The ∧ always points uphill in a canyon. The opposite, or ∨, points downhill along ridgelines. The best way to remember this is to find a peak summit on the map—which will be shown by a contour line forming a complete circle with the elevation given. Canyons and ridges will alternate next to each other, sloping away from the summit. It is like looking at the ground from 30,000 feet up in an airplane.

When you have learned to recognize natural features on a topographical map, there is little need for a compass. You would need one, however, if you encountered heavy, vision-impairing snow, heavily timbered country, or flatland with no visible landmarks.

Now, just for practice, you want to line up the map with a compass and thereby assure yourself that you are aligned with the terrain features. You must take magnetic declination into consideration. Magnetic declination simply means that a compass needle does not point to true north, but toward the magnetic field located near the North Pole. There are two lines on the bottom of the topographical map that point in the two directions: magnetic north which is compass north, and grid (true) north which is the way the map is oriented. Your compass will not give you a true orientation to the map until you compensate for this difference. The best way to do this is to line up a straight edge with the MN or magnetic north line. Draw a light pencil mark through the entire map following this line. Now place the compass on the map so that the needle lies along the pencil line. Let's say you see on your map that the declination is 13½ degrees. Turn the compass 13½ degrees to the left, or west. The N on the compass will now point to grid (true) north and be oriented with your map, and both will be oriented with the actual terrain features. For more detailed discussion of map and compass work, refer to the reading list in Appendix 2.

On the Trail—Keep Oriented

Everything checks out and you are chomping at the bit to get to Fremont Saddle where the breathtaking view of Weaver's Needle will greet you. It is decided that everyone will space out about 20 yards apart on the trail. This method of hiking gives each person a feeling of solitude and communication

Learn to use terrain features for orientation so that you could retrace your footsteps—even at night—if an emergency arose. Photo by Dave Ganci.

with the environment. You are the leader, and will be setting a leisurely pace.

Bodies warm up quickly due to the heat-producing exertion as you head up the trail. Boots don't fit as snugly as they did when the group started out. The watch says 8:00 A.M. and you take a gear adjustment break. This allows everyone to adjust to the temperature of the trail by removing or adding clothing; it allows tightening of bootlaces, shoulder straps, and belts. Since the temperature has climbed to about seventy-five degrees, you remove your wool sweater and unbutton the front of your cotton shirt for ventilation. You replace your wool pullover cap with a cool, shade-producing, felt hat.

The map shows a trail that zigzags back and forth across the dry streambed of Peralta Canyon. You glance up on either side of the canyon to find identifying landmarks. You have been on trail for a half hour and have traveled a horizontal distance of about a mile. You quickly measure out a mile on the map. You should be somewhere between Peaks 3694 and 4036 on the west, and just about opposite Peak 3445 on the east side of the canyon. You pick out anything prominent along the canyon sides that matches up to the map—needles, side canyons, caves. You look straight ahead and upward. There is a large cavelike opening at the top of the ridge. It is marked on the map as Geronimo Cave. Now you can pretty well pinpoint yourself on the map, even from down inside a canyon, the toughest place to orient from.

You're off again and feeling great. You ate a good breakfast and now you feel your blood circulating and your lungs exchanging polluted city air for some fresh, crisp wilderness air.

There's a ruckus up ahead. It's a horse packing outfit and they are heading down the canyon trail. Your group steps off the trail on the uphill side allowing them to pass. This is common trail courtesy everywhere. The cowboys look at you like you're crazy, and you look at them like they're lazy. They are carrying six-shooters on their hips, as is still done in much of the Superstition Wilderness.

Geronimo Cave is off to the right now, and you can spot the zigzag switchbacks that lead to Fremont Saddle up ahead. It is close to 9:00 A.M. and a pack break is in order. This short intermission will again allow everyone to readjust, slosh down some water, or take photos. This is a good time to glance back over the trail and make a mental note of the way a return trip down this same canyon would look. Even though you will be making a loop trip, and don't plan to come back down this trail, there is always the possibility of an emergency evacuation when you might have to lead a litter-carrying group out this trail—maybe even at night. These mental notes for a return trip should be made at every rest stop, fixing the image of prominent landmarks in the mind's eye. If you make this a

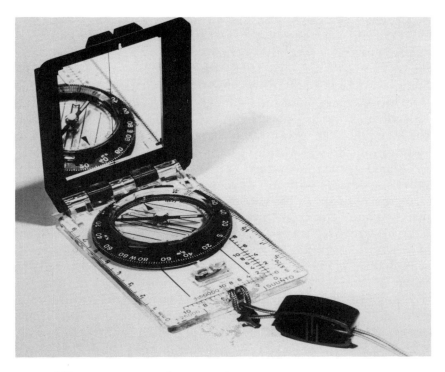

Suunto field compass. Courtesy of Suunto USA.

habit, you will never get lost, even when hiking off trail or cross-country with no compass.

Energy Conservation

The steep switchbacks now call for a slower pace, the secret of energy conservation. Energy conservation is a most important consideration for every wilderness trek, especially long, multi-day journeys.

I first became fully aware of energy conservation while attending the National Outdoor Leadership School educator's course. Paul Petzoldt, founder of NOLS, is a living example

of the energy conservation technique. He believes, as I do, that
if there are any secrets to efficient wilderness travel and
enjoyment, they are the principles of prior planning and
energy conservation. In 1938, Petzoldt climbed high on the
flanks of K2, the second highest mountain in the world. He
used no oxygen tanks and did not suffer the effects of high
altitude sickness, so prominent an affliction at those altitudes.
In fact, he felt great. Due to the illness of a climbing
companion, he was climbing alone, and at an altitude of close
to 27,000 feet he retreated. He had gone higher than any
previous person without oxygen. He credits that feat, along
with many more in his career, to the wise conservation of his
own strength and techniques of good camping procedures. He
has subsequently incorporated these into his outdoor leadership school.

Basically energy conservation means pacing yourself to
make the most efficient use of your energies. And that means
resisting the temptation to push yourself so hard toward your
goal that you become exhausted in the process. Becoming
overtired can lead to accident, injury, disharmony, bickering
within a group, sloppy camping procedures, and a negative
attitude toward the wilderness in general. Energy conservation
means setting a pace that makes hiking enjoyable and refreshing. It means arriving at your destination with plenty of time
and energy to set up camp and enjoy the evening. It means
maintaining a steady breathing rate while on the trail by
shifting into low gear, taking short, easy steps, and resting
often during steep climbs. It means snacking along the way
whenever you are hungry or thirsty. It means stopping whenever you feel uncomfortable—to adjust gear, to change clothing, or to put some tape over that hot spot on your foot. It
means that wilderness travel should not be a demonstration of
machismo but an enjoyable, well-planned interaction with the
natural elements.

All right, your low gear has carried you up the switchbacks
and Fremont Saddle is in sight. As you come up over the last
rise, the sight of Weaver's Needle jutting 1,200 feet straight up

from the desert floor makes your heart jump. It is 9:45 A.M. and you decide to take that half hour break here and soak up the view. Besides, it's time for a foot rub. You glance back along the trail and pick out Peralta Campground.

The temperature is eighty degrees but the weather report says it will get into the nineties by midafternoon. And since the rest of the day's travel will be mostly on open trail you decide to change into shorts. You focus the binoculars along the proposed route down East Boulder Canyon, looking for water holes. Even though each of you is carrying more than a gallon of water, you want to be aware of all the water sources available in the event of an emergency. The binoculars carry your gaze to Black Top Mesa on the east and Palomino Mountain on the west side of East Boulder Creek. Your eyes are getting heavy, so you lean up against the pack and close them. The soft spring breeze carries the scent of desert blossoms.

Clomp, clomp! You wake with a start. A couple of horseback riders are crossing the Saddle. It's 10:30 A.M., a half hour behind schedule. That's all right though, because there will be plenty of time left when you reach camp.

Leadership

It's time to play leader and see how everybody is doing. Any blisters? Pack problems? Sore muscles? Remember, since you are the leader, the buck stops with you. You must be able to see how every small circumstance fits into the big picture, and how it will affect the day's outcome. Although you take into consideration all the trip members' preferences, you will make all the final decisions regarding the safe, enjoyable conduct of the journey while considering all aspects of conserving the environment.

Everyone is refreshed and energized and ready to head down the trail to the first night's camp. There is no problem with landmarks now because Weaver's Needle will command the

skyline for the rest of the afternoon. Since Black Top Mesa
and Palomino Mountain are so prominent, you can have fun
with your family on the trail by making a game of letting
each person try to pick your exact location on the map. The
idea of making games out of your experiences solidifies and
brings harmony to a group, blending different personalities
into the striving for a common goal. This brings up the
element of group behavior in the wilderness. It is worth
thinking about because human nature can influence the
outcome of an outing just as sure as planning, equipment,
food, or survival techniques. In fact, human nature can pose
the toughest of all problems for a leader.

As long as everyone is having a good time, human nature is
all smiles. But let a crisis occur and the men are separated
from the boys; the weak separated from the strong; the savage
from the civilized man. This is one illustration of why
planning and preparation are so important: they help the trip
run smoothly. Something as simple as being too tired can
turn an otherwise enthusiastic, good-natured individual into a
dissatisfied tyrant. The elements of stress and pressure, fear
and fatigue, can turn friend against friend, brother against
brother, husband against wife. The thin veneer of civilized
behavior rubs away quickly after a couple of days of roughing
it in the wilderness. Everyone is in the same boat, or canyon,
as it were. And you, the leader, must be the negotiator in all
human conflicts on the trip.

The key to controlling these situations is maintaining your
self-control and setting the example of unselfishness. The
welfare of the group comes first; the goal of the trip stands in
second place. As leader, you must push your ego into the
background. At the same time, your role as leader must be
emphasized, in a pleasant way, from the start of the trip. It is
your responsibility to set the tone and pace of the trip and to
make every effort to keep all trip members comfortable. The
stresses and unknowns of wilderness travel dictate that you go
to all lengths possible to achieve compromises and get everybody working together. A good sense of humor is probably the

greatest asset a leader can have. It can make a tense situation into a funny one. It can keep spirits high and the group cohesive.

Good Camping

Even though you have kept a leisurely pace and stopped at 11:30 A.M. for a rest, it is only 1:30 P.M. when you pass the end of Palomino Mountain and come out on the open, flat area near which you had planned to make camp. You drop your packs and find some shady mesquite trees to sit under while you talk over good camping procedures. You have already set a good example by arriving at the present campsite in the early afternoon. It is better to leave extra early in the morning than to arrive in the dark. Camp location should be the first subject of discussion. Tents should be set up away from trails, streams, lakes, rivers—all bodies of water. If water must be secured from these sources, you will have to carry water containers to and from the source. Animals drink from these same sources, so campers should situate themselves far enough away to allow undisturbed access by wild creatures.

Courtesy and aesthetic values are also involved in campsite location. You should strive to camp away from other groups or individuals. They are trying to avoid the crowds, too, and since they have first rights to the location, you are obligated to move on, at least out of sight and sound. Pitch tents far enough away from trails to be hidden from view. Tents in the same party should also be located away from one another to allow personal privacy. When you see a beautiful spot, camp away from it and still enjoy the beauty. If you camp in the middle of it, it is no longer beautiful. It is "developed."

Think about safety too. Beware of camping at the base of steep cliffs where rockfall has occurred. Pitch tents and tarps at least 40 feet away from the kitchen area. If there is a prevailing wind, pitch shelters upwind from campfires. And pitch your roof so that same prevailing wind is blowing from the rear. Stay out of drainages.

Try to clear as little as possible for the tent site. Keep the tent area clean and uncluttered. When the camp is broken, make the spot look as if no one had been there. All litter should be carried out. Burying garbage is an invitation for animals to dig it up. Burn all papers in the fire pit, but remember that anything with plastic or aluminum foil will not burn up. Carry it out. If you're gathering firewood, do it before dark. If you ever step on a pincushion cactus or bump into a cholla after dark, you'll know why.

Water Holes

The hottest part of the desert day is past. Water must be secured now, so your group will take a hike up Little Boulder Canyon to look for seeps.

"Snort, snort! Snuffle!"

Everyone freezes. A quick brown flash darts by about 20 yards away. Then another. And another. Javelinas—the peccary of the desert. You've surprised them, but now they've caught your scent. They disappear over the ridge one by one, about 30 seconds apart. You find the spot where they have been digging for roots, at the base of some prickly pear pads.

All litter should be carried out, even that left behind by others. Photo by Dave Ganci.

Use a small, rubberized canvas or plastic bucket for bathing. Photo by Dave Ganci.

You move further up the canyon.

"Hey," your son shouts. "A water hole."

A small stream trickles into a deep cache basin, flows a short way downhill, then disappears against the side of the creekbed. The pool is deep enough to dip a gallon container into. You fill all four and tell your family a bit about water holes. You mention the fact that animals and insects use these mini-oases also, and there can be no justification for polluting any water source. Latrines should always be located far away from water, just like tent sites. The water hole is the most important piece of real estate in the desert. No one has exclusive rights to it. Hikers should avoid special catch basins that have been built by game and fish departments. These basins were built because water was in short supply for wildlife, so they have priority—unless emergency situations exist.

Keep It Clean

On the way back to the campsite, your group picks up some dead mesquite branches for firewood. While heating some water for tea, you start thinking about camp cleanliness.

There is no real need for soap on a weekend backpack. You can wash kitchen utensils in plain hot water for a couple days. You can use plain water for hand and face rinsing too. You can stand yourself without a bath for a weekend. If you just have to have a bath, take along a rubber-coated canvas bucket. Dip it into a water source and carry it *away* from that source. Pour it over your head and hold your breath. A GI bath for sure, but this method prevents polluting.

If the trip extends into a multiday journey, bathing becomes more justified. You can still use the bucket method for washing. You still do not need soap, however. Water alone will wash off most of the grime and body salts. Save the Zest for the bathtub.

If you find a water source such as a free-running stream and you are hot and sweaty after a long day, a cool dip feels heavenly. But no soap. If you find only water holes that are not part of any free-running system, there should be no bathing except with the bucket method. They may be the only water sources for local wildlife. There is no justification for ever dumping or dunking any foreign material, including food, into a water source. It would be like washing your underwear in your neighbor's drinking well.

On an extended trip, soap for hand washing is advisable, especially after latrine use. Biodegradable dishwashing soap becomes practical on an extended trip, also. You can get your hands clean by volunteering for pot washing.

Clothes washing needs no soap. Socks and underwear are the only items of clothing normally washed on backpack trips. Plain water will rinse most of the dirt and salts out. You can wash them with soap when you get home.

Latrines

You have brought your metal trowel along to dig holes in that tough desert soil. Plastic shovels will break. In soft soil, a common latrine can be dug. It can be anywhere from one to two feet deep, one foot wide, and two feet long. In many desert soils, a common latrine is too difficult to dig, therefore individual cat holes are the solution. These should be at least six inches deep.

I realize this will be highly controversial, but consider this innovation: no toilet paper! When you get the call, simply gather a collection of small stones, twigs, dried plant material, grasses if available, and leaves if you know what they are. After making your deposit and using up your little pile of natural aids, push the soil back over the hole and walk away. Voila! No toilet paper to burn or to be dug up by desert dwellers. None to carry—or forget. None to visually pollute the desert landscape.

Do you realize how far away pieces of toilet paper can be seen on the desert? Just like shiny beer cans, they can be spotted for miles. And just like beer cans, they preserve well.

Most people's attitude toward latrine duty is that it is a necessary evil, best accomplished in a hurry and just as quickly disregarded. But it is just as much a part of life as eating, sleeping, loving, and walking. We simply produce a waste product that should be disposed of in a manner which leaves no trace. There is a small group of us desert rats that practice this paperless ethic on the barren lands. If it can be done there, it can be done anywhere. In wetter, lusher environments, there is an unlimited supply of leaves and grasses. A side benefit is that you'll be learning plant identification while on the john, rather than reading a comic book. You may laugh, but I have not used toilet paper in the wilderness in years. And no, I don't hike alone a lot.

Your latrine location should be on high ground away from drainages and campsites. In any group situation, a designated spot or general area should be set up with the above rules in mind. Everyone should be briefed on the traceless sanitation approach. If you are not yet liberated, and feel the need for toilet paper, you must burn it after use. That means another thing you must carry on your person at all times: matches.

Urination usually doesn't require as stringent an approach, but the high ground and drainage rules still apply. I have to be the first to admit how uncomfortable it is to get up on a cold night with bladder ready to burst, stumble into your moccasins, fumble with the flashlight, trip over a dead saguaro branch, check the wind direction, and then release. The point is to get away from camp, even if you are camped in the snow. Hot tea is a bit tangy if a trace of yellow snow has been inadvertently melted along with the water.

I won't go into any story details here, but I'll just relate that in emergency situations, I have used plastic bags, bottles, and rubber boots (I'll never live that one down). On Mt. McKinley in Alaska, I was wearing a pair of undershorts, a pair of longjohns, wool pants, down pants, and wind pants. With a blizzard howling, I had to release my bladder. It wasn't until I zipped up that I realized I hadn't made it past the wool. Male anatomy tends to shrink, trying to stay warm in sub-zero temperatures.

Keeping a Journal

After dinner has been cooked and eaten, everyone heads for his sleeping bag. It's been a long day full of new sights and experiences and you want to get up early in the morning so you can catch the sunrise. But before you go to sleep, you want to record the highlights of the day in your journal. Jotting down each day's adventures and tying them in to the photographs you have taken will become a story of your trip. Your family will treasure this record of your time together.

Keeping a journal is fun but it also serves a very practical purpose. By keeping notes on your time and distance you will be able to see how accurately you have planned the trip and at the same time have more tangible information to work with when you plan your next trip. Records of the wildlife and plants you have seen along the way will enhance your appreciation of the desert environment. Make a special point of jotting down brief descriptions of the plants and animals you do not recognize while your memory of how they looked is still fresh. When you get back to civilization you can look them up at the library or another source so that you will know what they are the next time you see them.

Other valuable journal entries are notes on how useful or useless, how convenient or inconvenient various pieces of equipment proved to be. Then when you plan your next trip you'll be better able to decide what gear, food, or clothing should be added or subtracted to suit your family's preferences and needs.

The hike in is just a start. The next day will be a rest day and a time for feeling the desert experience. You doze off under clear skies, getting recharged for. . . .

10

A Day in the Desert

. . . I might as well take a siesta—everything else does.

Dawn

Bzzt! Yawn. Your wristwatch alarm tells you it's 4:00 A.M. Yawn. You start to doze off and are slightly awakened by the soft cooing of doves, and then brusquely awakened by the tat-a-tat of the cactus wren. Soon a symphony of birdcalls, including the mockingbird's and the quail's, keeps you awake now. They are carrying on early morning conversation as they head for water. Birds are the desert's alarm clock.

You rouse your family and put on your woolies. It is the coolest part of the day. You heat up some tea to get yourselves going and to wash down the granola you'll eat for breakfast.

First light is appearing as you head for Boulder Canyon. It is silver light, cold light, and it dims the starlight. The rocks and sand around you have released their heat energy during the night. Everything is still. Lizards, snakes, and toads are buried in the sand, in crevices and in holes under the desert floor. Their bodies are not warm-blooded so they must wait until things warm up before they can start their day.

While you all were sleeping back at camp, other warm-blooded animals were prowling the night in their endless

143

Mourning dove, Zenaidura macroura, *nesting in Cardon cactus. Courtesy of the Desert Botanical Garden.*

search for one another. Now that dawn is approaching, the coyote, bobcat, fox, civet cat, and skunk are on the lookout for last minute snacks before the heat of the day forces them into rest and shade. Deer that had come down from the upper ranges during the night for warmth and water, are heading back up to cool country. Javelinas are snuffling and digging for prickly pear fruits and roots.

The predawn colors are now on display: pink, green, silver, and red shafts of light pulling the sun up over the horizon. As the first orange rays cast long, eerie, black shadows, the desert day shift begins. The temperature changes that will occur during the next 24 hours will be more extreme than those of any other natural habitat on earth. There may be differences of as much as eighty degrees, more than twice the average daily temperature variation in the United States. These extremes have led to the tremendous varieties of desert plants and animals. Millions of evolutionary years have taught these living things to react instinctively to the extremes of heat and cold.

Audubon Cara-cara, a bird of prey that flies southward from the Lower Sonoran Desert. Courtesy of Phoenix Zoo.

Wily coyote, Canis latrans, *survives against trememdous odds. They are extremely adaptable; and many are seen in the Phoenix area. Courtesy of Phoenix Zoo.*

Morning

In Boulder Canyon you stretch out on your foam pads and focus your binoculars on the water holes. You observe the early morning drinkers obeying the rules of their bondage to the desert environment. The doves and quail are there. Their day is beginning. The owl, badger, ring-tailed cat, coyote, and bobcat tank up before heading for their burrows. Their day is ending.

The night-blooming cereus flowers are closing shop for the day, while soft-winged moths are starting to fold up and cling to the undersides of the cereus leaves to wait out the day in the shade.

You are getting warm already, and you take off the wool sweater. You look at your watch. It is 7:00 A.M. and the heat is climbing quickly. The business of life on the desert will soon slow down to a crawl. But the birds will remain active all day. Flight keeps them cool and most of them have body temperatures between 104 and 108 degrees anyway.

Swoosh! Shriek! A gila woodpecker flashes by and lands on

Desert bighorn sheep, usually found in isolated desert mountain ranges. Courtesy of Phoenix Zoo.

(Left) Sparrow who has taken over a saguaro boot for his home. Chances are this hole was made by a gila woodpecker while searching for beetles to eat. Courtesy of Phoenix Zoo.

(Right) The coati or chulla, Nasua narica, lives in Mexico, Arizona, and New Mexico. Seen most often in desert mountains, these entertaining rascals travel in groups along the ground or through trees. The range of their diet is extensive. My brother owned one once, and it ate his couch. Courtesy of Phoenix Zoo.

a saguaro. You recognize him by his red cap and his black and white wings. He begins pecking holes in the cactus. He is feeding himself on insect larvae while cleaning the cactus of destructive parasites and carving holes big enough for nesting places. Sparrow hawks, screech owls, gilded flickers, fly-catchers, and other hole-nesting animals will avail themselves of these free apartments.

This interrelationship among birds, plants, and insects is a good example of the vital connections of all living things to one another. By satisfying its own needs, and no more than that, each animal performs services for other animals and plants. The life chain is perpetuated.

The sun is getting higher. The air and the ground are heating up fast. You notice some of the plants around you. As you lie in the shade of a mesquite tree you observe how spread out it is on the desert floor and how tiny are its leaves. The saguaro, cholla, prickly pear, ocotillo, and palo verde are all spread out with spaces of open ground in between as if to say, "This is my property. Stay out." Their seeming isolation is

due to lack of water. It is first-come, first-served, on the desert, and when a seed is lucky enough to sprout and take root in a particular patch of clear ground, it usually has priority on the water in that spot until it dies.

Your gaze goes from the distant horizon of endless cacti to the ground in front of you. You notice a strong-jawed, spiderlike solpugid excavating a burrow. You watch a bright scarlet velvet ant, the adult female of a certain species of wasp, racing toward her home underground. These insects, like rodents, lizards. spiders, and other burrowing creatures, aerate the hard desert soil to allow the infrequent rainstorms to penetrate the tough ground and provide plant roots with water. By the way, those pretty, multicolored velvet ants are supposed to have the worst sting, gram for gram, of any member of the wasp family.

A swift movement catches the corner of your eye. It stops cold. It is the cocky, fearless, roadrunner. He has a lizard dangling from his beak. That reminds you of lunchtime. It is close to 11:00 A.M. and the heat is getting heavy. You pick up

The roadrunner, Geococcyx californianus, is a member of the cuckoo family. Its diet includes lizards, insects, and snakes. It kills and eats rattlesnakes by giving them sharp blows on the head. They are frequently seen zooming across the highways in desert areas. They fly only short distances. Courtesy of Phoenix Zoo.

your day packs and head back to camp as the sun approaches its zenith.

After lunch you feel sleepy. You take one last look out at the shimmering, glaring desert floor. No shadows now. No movement, no sounds save a few birds, cicadas, and harvester ants.

Everything seems to have decided it is siesta time. So do you. It felt cool and comfortable in the early morning, but now you would just as soon sleep through the heat in this nice, shady spot because you know the highest temperatures are yet to come. By 2:00 or 3:00 P.M. the heat will be at its maximum and you wonder how anything can survive the 100-degree-plus temperatures out there. But then everything is either underground, in a tree, under a rock, in the shade of a cactus or cave, or, like you, in the shade of a mesquite tree. You, along with the rattlesnake, horned toad, moth, gila monster, gecko, tortoise, and rabbit, are safe from the sun.

Afternoon

Suddenly the sun shining from a low angle underneath the mesquite branches strikes your eyes and awakens you. It is 5:00 P.M. You have slept away the afternoon. But there are countless other desert creatures that have slept it away also. You heat up some desert stew and spread some green chili jelly on a slice of zucchini bread. After finishing off some ephedra tea, you fill your canteens and head back out to the observation spot.

The sun is nearing the horizon. A furry tarantula meanders across your path and disappears down into its underground cave. The desert seems to be coming alive now. More birds are flitting about. More insects are trying to dodge them. A covey of quail darts along ahead, going for the water hole. You find the mesquite trees and get comfortable again. The sun is setting and the scene captures your family's attention for nearly an hour. Blazing oranges, blues, purples, reds, yellows, fade into scarlet and crimson.

Night

You reach for the binoculars and spot a striped skunk ambling up to the water hole. The desert night has begun. Many of the desert creatures must secure water during the early evening hours because of the strict bondage of narrow temperature ranges in which they can survive. The desert becomes a frantic who-eats-whom battleground during these hours. The night creatures are driven from their hiding places by hunger and thirst, in search of seeds, roots, pollen, and one another.

(Above) Rock rattler, Crotalus lepidus. *Inhabits the upper edge of desert grassland. Courtesy of Phoenix Zoo.*

(Right) Western diamondback, Crotalus atrox. *Favors warm desert and grasslands. It's mostly nocturnal during the summer. A very wary, nervous, and highly defensive critter. Courtesy of Phoenix Zoo.*

Insects eat pollen. Rodents eat insects. Reptiles eat rodents. Owls eat reptiles. And so it goes, the never-ending cycle that assures the perpetuation of all species of life.

It is getting cooler now; time to get sweaters and vests out again. You turn on your flashlight and notice a walking stick and a praying mantis on the branch in front of you. You hear wild bees. They are heading for the pollen in the evening primrose. A couple of wood rats dash away from the light. They were contemplating a route to the package of cheese and crackers stuffed in the side pocket of your day pack. The flashlight reveals the white blossom of the cereus. It blooms at night to seduce the hungry night-flying insects that will pollinate its flowers as they feed on its nectar.

You and your family are becoming increasingly aware of the fact that nature is an incredibly complex system of unending interdependencies involving more factors than man can account for. All living things depend on their habitat—soil,

water, climate, air, and other animals—to sustain their life cycles. If something disrupts the cycles in this habitat for very long, the life within it dies. The cycle of life and death perpetuates the earth's ability to replenish life-giving substances from the substances released in death. You begin to put into perspective man's attempt to change and control the forces of nature and realize why so many control campaigns have backfired.

Your watch tells you it's 8:00 P.M. and you doze off. Those little rock rats move in. They gnaw through your pack and your plastic baggies. They fill up on your food supply and dash away. One makes it back to his underground cave. The other is nabbed by a hungry owl who has been watching patiently from the saguaro not too far away.

You are awakened by the gila woodpecker. You notice the hole in your pack and start to holler. Then you realize that you were within the boundaries of some other creature's

Great horned owl, Bubo virginianus. *Prevalent throughout the U.S. Eats rodents and small mammals. Courtesy of Phoenix Zoo.*

habitat, and that during the night you became, if ever so slightly, part of the never-ending food chain.

You return to camp and discuss the next day's hike back to Peralta Campground by way of the Needle Trail. After the discussion, everyone sacks out and you decide to record the day's adventures in your journal. It has been a day you want to remember.

Appendix 1:
Starting Points

We live in a country that has pioneered the concept of putting aside, for all time, certain natural areas as sanctuaries for endangered wildlife species and as sites of special scenic, historic, or scientific value. The desert is no exception. What follows here is a list of some of these protected desert areas and brief descriptions of their special features and facilities. Mailing addresses have been included so that you can write them for more detailed information. It is hoped that the knowledge and insight you gain from visiting some of the desert areas will enhance both your appreciation of their unique beauty and your pleasure in exploring them.

Chihuahuan Desert

Big Bend National Park, 708,000 acres. Backcountry camping, picnicking. Information center, interpretive programs, groceries and service station, lodge providing meals and overnight accommodations. Write Big Bend National Park, Texas 79834.

Guadalupe Mountains National Park, 79,000 acres. Information

157

Fig. 1.

Key to Map Numbers
1 Big Bend National Park
2 Guadalupe Mountains; Carlsbad Caverns
   National Parks
3 White Sands National Monument
4 Bosque del Apache National Wildlife
   Refuge
5 Chiricahua Mountains
6 Saguaro National Monument
7 Aravaipa Canyon
8 Organ Pipe Cactus National Monument
9 Joshua Forest Parkway
10 Kofa Game Range
11 Algodones Dunes
12 Anza; Borrego Desert State Park
13 Joshua Tree National Monument
14 Antelope Valley
15 Owens Valley
16 Death Valley National Monument
17 Desert National Wildlife Range
18 Valley of Fire State Park; Lake Mead
   National Recreation Area
19 Grand Canyon National Park
20 Cathedral Gorge State Park
21 Wheeler Peak
22 Great Salt Lake; Bear River Migratory Bird
   Refuge
23 Ruby Lake National Wildlife Refuge
24 Pyramid Lake
25 Stillwater Marshes
26 Mono Lake
27 Malheur National Wildlife Refuge
28 Charles Sheldon Antelope Refuge
29 Hart Mountain National Antelope Refuge

office and many backcountry trails. Write Superintendent, Carlsbad Caverns National Park, 3225 National Parks Hwy, Carlsbad, New Mexico 88220.

Carlsbad Caverns National Park, 46,00 acres. Self-guiding nature trails, backcountry trails, and of course, the Caverns themselves. Overnight accommodations in White City and Carlsbad, New Mexico. Write 3225 National Parks Hwy, Carlsbad, New Mexico 88220.

Chiricahua National Monument, 10,700 acres. Paved roads, camping and picnic areas, trails, information center, overnight accommodations. Write Dos Cabezas Star Route, Box 6500, Willcox, Arizona 85643.

White Sands National Monument, 140,000 acres. Scenic drive, picnic area, and information center. Write Box 458, Alamagordo, New Mexico 88310.

Bosque del Apache National Wildlife Refuge, 57,000 acres. Gravel tour road and information booth. Write Box 278, San Antonio, New Mexico 87832.

Sitting Bull Canyon and Falls. Trails and picnic and camping areas. Write Federal Building, 11th and New York, Alamagordo, New Mexico 88310.

Arizona Sonoran Desert

Aravaipa Canyon. Protected nature sanctuary in southern Arizona; limited access permits. Write Defenders of Wildlife, 3rd Floor, United Bank Building, 120 W. Broadway, Tucson, Arizona 85701.

Superstition Mountains. Desert wilderness area with many trails, unique topography. Site of legendary Lost Dutchman Mine, located 30 miles east of Phoenix. Write Tonto National Forest, Room 6428, Federal Building, 230 N. 1st Avenue., Phoenix, Arizona 85025.

Saguaro National Monument, 77,000 acres. Divided into two units, east and west of Tucson, Arizona. Backcountry trails, nature trails, paved roads, picnic areas, information center. Write Rte. 8, Box 695, Tucson, Arizona 85730.

Sabino Canyon. Desert oasis located in the Santa Catalina Mountains northeast of Tucson. Trails, picnic areas, information center. Write Box 551, Tucson, Arizona 85702.

Cabeza Prieta National Game Range, 860,000 acres. Arid, wild desert area on Mexican border in southwestern Arizona. Sanctuary for bighorn sheep and pronghorn antelope. Limited access. Write Box 1032, Yuma, Arizona 85364.

Organ Pipe National Monument, 330,000 acres. Paved roads, campgrounds, and trails. Rte. 1, Box 100, Ajo, Arizona 85321.

Kofa National Game Range, 660,000 acres. Extremely arid desert in western Arizona. Desert bighorn sheep sanctuary, 4-wheel drive roads, gold mine country. Write Box 1032, Yuma, Arizona 85364.

Tonto National Monument, 1120 acres. Near Theodore Roosevelt Dam. Preserved Indian dwellings, trails, information center. Write Box 707, Roosevelt, Arizona 85545.

Arizona-Sonoran Desert Museum. Living museum of the plants and animal life 14 miles west of Tucson in Tucson Mountain Park.

Desert Botanical Garden of Arizona, 150 acres. Arboretum including about 3,800 plants from deserts of the world, located in Papago Park, Phoenix, Arizona.

Boyce Thompson Southwestern Arboretum. Riparian area of desert plants and bird life located 3 miles west of Superior, Arizona, on U.S. Highway 60.

Lake Mead Recreation Area, 1.9 million acres. Paved roads, camping and picnic areas, boat-launching ramps, boat rentals and excursions, jeep excursions, information center, meals, lodgings, service stations, groceries. Write 601 Nevada Highway, Boulder City, Nevada 89005.

Grand Canyon National Park, 1.2 million acres. Public mini-buses, interpretive programs, camping and picnic areas, full accommodations, hiking trails, river trips. Write Grand Canyon N.P., P.O. Box 129, Grand Canyon, Arizona 86023.

Heard Museum. Private museum of Indian arts and crafts located at 22 E. Monte Vista, Phoenix, Arizona.

Mohave Desert

Death Valley National Monument, 1.9 million acres. Paved roads, jeep trails, camping and picnic areas, full accommodations, interpretive programs, information center. Write Death Valley, California 92328.

Desert National Wildlife Range, 1.5 million acres. Limited picnic facilities and backroads, information center. Write 1500 N. Decatur Boulevard, Las Vegas, Nevada 89108.

Joshua Tree National Monument, 500,000 acres. Paved and gravel roads, camping and picnic areas, trails, information center. Write 74485 National Monument Dr., 29 Palms, California 92277.

Palm Springs Desert Museum. Exhibits of animals and plants, geology, climate, Indians of the California deserts located at East Tahquitz-McCallum Way in Palm Springs.

Barstow Way Station. Headquarters for the Bureau of Land Management's High Desert Resource Area. Interpretive information, exhibits, information center. Write Bureau of Land Management, 831 Barstow Road, Barstow, California 92311.

Huntington Botanical Gardens. Located on the estate of the Huntington Library and Art Gallery with 25,000 desert plant specimens from around the world. Write 1151 Oxford Road, San Marino, California.

Great Basin Desert

Ruby Lake National Wildlife Refuge, 37,600 acres. Resting and feeding area for migratory waterfowl; some roads, campground. Write Ruby Valley, Nevada 89833.

Wheeler Peak, 28,000 acres. Paved and gravel roads, camping and picnic areas, trails. Write Humboldt National Forest, Baker, Nevada 89311.

Bear River Migratory Bird Refuge, 65,000 acres. Gravel tour roads, picnic area. Write Box 459, Brigham City, Utah 84302.

Malheur National Wildlife Refuge, 181,000 acres. Paved and gravel roads, camping areas, information center. Write Box 113, Burns, Oregon 97720.

Hart Mountain National Antelope Refuge, 275,000 acres. Gravel roads, primitive camping, wilderness camping, information center. Write Box 111, Lakeview, Oregon 97630.

Colorado Desert

Anza-Borrego Desert State Park, 500,000 acres. Paved and gravel roads, 4-wheel drive trails, hiking trails, picnic areas, accommodations. Write Borrego Springs, California 92004.

Salton Sea National Wildlife Refuge. Wintering area for shorebirds, ducks, and geese. Write Box 247, Calipatria, California 92233.

Algodones Dunes, 200 square miles. Sand dunes in southeastern California. Write Bureau of Land Management, Federal Building, 2800 Cottage Way, Sacramento, California 95825.

Painted Desert

Petrified Forest National Park, 94,000 acres. Self-guiding interpretive drive, hiking trails. Write P.O. Box 217, Petrified Forest N.P., Arizona 86028.

Monument Valley Navajo Tribal Park, over 1 million acres. Dirt roads, camping and picnic areas, conducted 4-wheel drive trips. Write Arizona State Office of Tourism, 1100 W. Washington, Phoenix, Arizona 85007.

Appendix 2:
Information Sources

RECOMMENDED READING

Deserts in General

Butcher, Russell D. *The Desert*. The Viking Press, 1976

Cloudsley-Thompson, John. *The Desert*. London: Orbis Publishing, 1977

Costello, David E. *The Desert World*. New York: Thomas Y. Crowell Company, 1972

Findley, Rowe. *Great American Deserts*. National Geographic Society, 1972

Jaeger, Edmund C. *The North American Deserts*. Stanford University Press, 1967

Kirk, Ruth. *Desert, The American Southwest*. Houghton-Mifflin Co., 1973

Larson, Peggy. *Deserts of America*. Prentice-Hall, 1970

Leopold, A. Starker. *The Desert*. Time Incorporated, 1962

Porter, Eliot. *The Place No One Knew*. Ballantine Books, 1966

Sutton, Ann and Myron. *The Life of the Desert*. McGraw-Hill, 1966

Cookery

Barker, Harriet. *Supermarket Backpacker*. Greatlakes Living Press, 1977

Barker, Harriet. *The One-Burner Gourmet*. Greatlakes Living Press, 1975

Kinmont, Vikki and Axcell, Claudia. *Simple Foods for the Pack*. San Francisco: Sierra Club Books, 1976

Lappe, Frances Moore. *Diet For a Small Planet*. New York: Ballantine Books, 1971

Mendenhall, Ruth Dyar. *Backpack Cookery*. La Siesta Press, 1966

Pallister, Nancy, ed. *NOLS Cookery*. Emporia: Kansas State Teachers College Press, 1974

First Aid and Survival

Darvill, Fred T., M.D., *Mountaineering Medicine*. Wilderness Press, Berkeley, 1983.

Grant, Harvey and Murray, Robert. *Emergency Care*. Prentice-Hall, Inc., 1971

National Red Cross. *Standard First Aid and Personal Safety*. Doubleday and Company, Inc., 1973

Wilkerson, James A., ed. *Medicine for Mountaineering*. Seattle: Mountaineers, 1967

Philosophy and Planning

Fletcher, Colin. *The Man Who Walked Through Time*. New York: Alfred A. Knopf, 1967

Fletcher, Colin. *The New Complete Walker*. New York: Alfred A. Knopf, 1974.

Climbing Committee of the Mountaineers, *The Freedom of the Hills*. Seattle: Mountaineers, 1960

Petzoldt, Paul. *The Wilderness Handbook*. New York: W. W. Norton and Co., Inc., 1974

Saijo, Albert. *The Backpacker*. San Francisco: 101 Productions, 1972

Natural History of the Desert

Dodge, Natt N. *100 Desert Wildflowers in Natural Colors.* Globe, Arizona: Southwest Parks and Monuments Association, 1973

Olin, George. *Mammals of the Southwestern Deserts.* Globe: Southwest Parks and Monuments Association, 1954

Smith, Gusse Thomas. *Birds of the Southwestern Desert.* Scottsdale: Doubleshoe Publishers, 1973

SOURCES OF USGS TOPOGRAPHICAL MAPS

U.S. Geological Survey
Box 25286
Federal Bldg.
Denver, CO 80225

U.S. Geological Survey
345 Middlefield Road
Menlo Park, CA 94025

U.S. Geological Survey
536 National Center
Reston, VA 22092

Afterword

Stepping into the desert is like stepping into a time machine. The millions, even billions, of years of the earth's history are recorded in the eroded geology of the buttes, mesas, and canyons. Fossils can be found underfoot. Observing these can take us back to the times of the early trilobites, some of the first sea-life forms. The quiet and solitude of this geologic landscape provides a librarylike atmosphere for the desert traveler. Man's extremely short history on earth is put into proper perspective against the background of slow evolutionary change. The desert landscape is honest, open, clean, devoid of wasted motion and growth. It has been this way for millions of years. Even the thousands of years of Indian habitation changed it imperceptibly.

As hikers and backpackers, we can help protect the character of this special place. We can pass through these lands of little water unnoticed, leaving no trace of our sojourn. We can carry back memories, photographs, and stories to pass on to future backcountry enthusiasts who in turn can venture out and discover the desert for themselves. If all of us practice the

(Above) Cactus gardens scene at the Desert Botanical Garden in Phoenix. Courtesy of the Garden.
(Below) Painted Rocks State Historic Park is located southwest of Phoenix, near Gila Bend. It is an outstanding group of Indian rock-art drawings of lizards, men, and geometric figures. Courtesy of State Parks, Arizona.

The famous Weaver's Needle in Superstition Wilderness, 50 miles east of Phoenix. Courtesy U.S. Forest Service.

environmentally sound techniques explained in this book, 100 people can pass through an area and have less impact on it than a party of two unconcerned individuals.

Concern, then, is what it's all about. And one of my aims in this book has been to concern hikers and backpackers with the preservation, and hence the present and future enjoyment, of our desert treasures.

But hikers and backpackers are not alone in the quest for desert treasures. Rock hounds, bicyclists, birdwatchers, scientists, miners, horseback riders, motorcyclists, campers, painters, ranchers, and power line engineers are among those penetrating the solitude once reserved for only the hardiest of explorers.

Our country's 500,000 square miles of desert, ranging across California, Nevada, Arizona, Oregon, Utah, Idaho, New Mex-

Peeking at a rattler's den. Through glass-fronted simulated burrows, one may see desert dwellers like the kit fox, pack rat, and the ringtail cat in their daytime hiding places. Courtesy of Arizona Desert Sonora Museum.

ico, and Texas, represents one of our last reservoirs of open space, offering the desert explorer a lifetime of variety and splendor. Eventually all of it will come under study and land management programs. This means that all of us desert pedestrians must assume an ever-louder voice in the decisions regarding the future of these so-called wastelands. We must raise our voices in the cause of preservation. We must join conservation organizations. We must write editorials for our local newspapers. We must raise hell with our legislators. In order to be heard, we must get involved. If we don't, our lands of little water and infinite beauty will be lost.

Footprints

After burros pass,
on a dusty road . . .
footprints.

After you and I go down
the last trail . . .
footprints.

Brooms of the winds
sweep footprints
into dustheaps.

The above is William Haskell Simpson's poem, "Footprints," from *Along Old Trails*, p. 21. Boston—New York: Houghton Mifflin Co.,1929.

Index